Barbecues
SALADS AND PICNICS

PHOTOGRAPHY BY ROWAN FOTHERINGHAM
STYLING BY DONNA HAY

BayBooks

An imprint of HarperCollins*Publishers*

STOCKISTS

Accoutrement Cook Shop
611 Military Road
Mosman NSW Australia
Tel: (02) 969 1031

Country Road Homewear
427 Victoria Road
Chatswood NSW Australia
Tel: (02) 413 3754
(stores all over Australia)

Hale Imports
Pillivuyt
97–99 Old Pittwater Road
Brookvale NSW Australia
Tel: (02) 938 2400

Les Olivades
2 Transvaal Ave
Double Bay NSW Australia
Tel: (02) 327 8073

Orrefors Kosta Boda
Shop 1033 Westfield Shopping Centre
Miranda NSW Australia
Tel: (02) 524 9409

A BAY BOOKS PUBLICATION
Bay Books, an imprint of
HarperCollins*Publishers*
25 Ryde Road, Pymble, Sydney NSW 2073, Australia
Distributed in the United States of America by
HarperCollins Publishers
10 East 53rd Street, New York NY 10022, USA

First published in Australia in 1993
This edition published in the USA in 1995

ISBN 1 86378 255 9

Cover, chapter openers and some internal photography by Rowan Fotheringham
Food stylist: Donna Hay
Food stylist's assistant: Beth Pitman
Front cover photograph: Greek Brochettes (recipe page 25), Red Mullet in Corn Husks (recipe page 34)
Back cover photograph: Lobster with Cress and Balsamic Vinegar (recipe page 39)
Bowls from Orrefors Kosta Boda

Printed in China
9 8 7 6 5 4 3 2 1
99 98 97 96 95

CONTENTS

Eating Outdoors

What better way to enjoy the great outdoors than to barbecue a feast, entertain guests in the garden or pack a picnic? *Barbecues, Picnics and Salads* is packed with recipe ideas for all these occasions.

BARBECUE PERFECTION

To barbecue simply means to cook over an open fire. Over millennia, since fire was discovered, people have built some sort of fireplace to cook food — especially meat or fish. Today, barbecues are more popular than ever. The only problem is in choosing which kind best suits your needs.

Which Barbecue?

Barbecues come in many types and sizes ranging from the most basic firebowls to grills on wheels complete with griddles and rotisseries. Work out exactly what you want your barbecue for — decide on the size for your needs and whether you need a portable or a fixed one — set yourself a price limit and the rest should be plain sailing.

WHAT KIND OF BARBECUE? What do you plan to use your barbecue for? Obviously it is not worth investing in a top-of-the-line mobile barbecue if you eat outdoors only a couple of times a year. On the other hand, if you entertain frequently, it is equally poor value to buy a barbecue that's too small or flimsy and won't last the distance.

PORTABLE OR FIXED? A permanent barbecue is great if you entertain often or eat outdoors regularly, but it needs to be positioned for summer shade and winter sun. A portable barbecue — such as a smaller rectangular or bowl-shaped one — has the advantage that you can use it both for picnics and in your garden. You can also move it around to take advantage of the weather.

TYPE Grills, griddle or covered? If you simply want to barbecue on the grill then the widest range of barbecues is available, from the basic hibachi to a gas-fired mobile grill with all the features you can imagine. A griddle or hot plate can be useful for onions or small items, and many models combine both cooking surfaces. If you plant to entertain adventurously then you may want a rotisserie for spit-roasting. The increasingly popular covered barbecues, which can be used with the lid up for barbecuing, or closed for roasting and even smoking, lets you cook in the great outdoors in all kinds of weather.

SIZE Make sure that the cooking area is large enough for your needs. It is better to buy a little too big than too small as it is important to be able to serve everyone together when eating alfresco.

Fuel

WOOD Traditionally used for cooking, wood is not the best fuel for barbecuing because it burns with a flame. Barbecue cooking needs heat — not flames. It is essential to let flames die down leaving a bed of hot embers before cooking. All too often people light the fire and start barbecuing. We all know the rather charred results.

CHARCOAL Charcoal is essentially wood that has already been burned.

Always keep water close at hand. If a tap or hose is not accessible, keep a bucket of water beside the fire. A fire extinguisher is useful if you barbecue regularly.

- Use fire starters to help start your fire, not flammable liquids.

- Keep children away from the fire — and away from matches.

- Watch for sparks, particularly when the weather's been dry, or on windy days.

- Keep current with local fire conditions, through the newspaper or television news.

- Keep a first aid kit nearby.

- Make sure there is adequate room to cook and serve the food — this will minimize the likelihood of burns or scalds.

- If you are barbecuing in the country, clear an area first and make sure you put out the fire completely afterwards.

This greatly speeds up the process of turning your fuel into a glowing bed of heat. It is the most effective fuel for barbecuing because:

- it provides plenty of heat,
- it is ready in 15 to 20 minutes,
- there's no smell,
- it can be bought in bags from the local supermarket or hardware store, and
- fatty flare-ups are not a problem because you can 'damp' to control the temperature.

PROPANE Gas barbecues tend to be more expensive but their big attraction is obviously their convenience: you can start barbecuing almost immediately. With the introduction of volcanic rock, gas barbecues have become even more popular. The rock is spread out below the cooking surface, absorbing the heat from the burners and glowing just like charcoal. This not only spreads the heat over a larger area but gives food an authentic barbecue flavor. Gas barbecues just couldn't be easier to operate: you simply connect the propane tank and turn on. It is always a good idea to keep a spare tank on hand in case the gas runs out. However, you can't use the damping technique to 'moisturize' food while cooking unless the burners are protected by a metal shield.

ELECTRICITY Electric barbecues are great for apartment dwellers. But they do have limited application because of the necessary outlets. Electric barbecues can also be combined with volcanic rock for that more authentic flavor.

Other Features to Consider

STABILITY It is essential to buy a barbecue that stands squarely on the ground. Top-of-the-line mobile grills provide the maximum stability in portables, but they are also the most expensive. Smaller portables or portables with detachable or fold-away legs tend to be less stable. Check the angle of the legs and overall stability before you buy. Table models need to be looked at with the same care, although most have very short legs or supports, and are quite stable.

COOKING HEIGHT Many barbecues have a cooking surface too close to coals. We recommend it should be at least 9 to 14 inches above the source of the heat: an adjustable height cooking surface is probably a good buy.

MATERIALS If your barbecue lives outdoors, make sure it is made of materials that won't rust away too readily. Alternatively, invest in a cover or put the portable barbecue in the garden shed.

SHELVES From the can of beer to food and sauces, you need plenty of space for putting things when barbecuing. Extra space never goes amiss, but a table alongside will do the trick. Warming racks above the barbecue are also useful, but not essential.

Barbecue Cooking Techniques

There are a variety of ways to cook a barbecue, from grilling, the most popular technique, through to spit-roasting. Try wrapping vegetables in foil and putting them in the hot embers to cook, or cooking shellfish in their shells — it's delicious!

BARBECUING Cooking food on a grill over the heat remains the most popular technique. Most of us have fond memories of succulent pieces of steak right off the grill. The basic principles are to cook with heat, not flame, and to retain the natural juices inside the food. Turning constantly allows the juices that run under heat to baste the food naturally. Any juices and fat which do drip fall on the fire, vaporize, and are absorbed back in the meat, adding a flavor which is unique to food barbecued in this way.

It doesn't take long to barbecue foods that are up to 2 inches thick and lie flat on the barbecue, or which can be cooked in wire barbecue baskets. Larger pieces of meat can be barbecued on the grill but need to be turned constantly and watched carefully so that the outside does not burn during the longer cooking time required.

The damping technique, plus constant turning, ensures that food is juicy when cooked. Don't overcook. Remember that your meat, fish or poultry will continue cooking in its own heat when taken off the barbecue. So remove just before it's ready.

GRIDDLE With griddle cooking it is the heat of the plate that cooks food rather than the direct heat of the fire. A thick plate will take longer to heat up, but will hold the heat longer than a thin one. It will also be less affected by the changes in the fire underneath, but consequently less responsive.

Essentially, using a griddle means that you are frying your food. It is most important to have good drainage for the fat and not underestimate how much there will be. Good drainage eliminates the risk of fat running on the fire, or building up and virtually deep-frying the food. If you want to fry onions or eggs on your barbecue a skillet will do the job just as well.

DAMPING

Damping is essential for successful barbecuing. Damp the fire with water either from a very fine spray from your hose or a spray bottle or by carefully sprinkling about a cup of water over the coals. This not only decreases the temperature immediately but it puts moisture back into the food with rising steam. If your barbecue grill is rather close to the coals you may wish to move the food aside as you spray or sprinkle. Do not damp down a gas barbecue unless there is a steel shield covering the burners.

FOIL Vegetables in foil are popular — particularly potatoes and corn. Use heavy-duty foil or two layers and wrap food with the dull side of the foil on the outside. Place parcels on the grill and turn while cooking. Potatoes are great when wrapped in foil and placed in the embers, as is corn on the cob, left in the husks.

SKEWERS Everything from meat, poultry and fish to fruit or vegetables can be cooked kebab-style on skewers. Cut meat into same-sized pieces. Remember, with beef or lamb kebabs, cook them later for those who like them rare.

The type of skewers you use is important. Choose flat ones with a diamond-shape end so that the food will stay on the skewer and will not roll around when turned.

Kebab turners come battery-operated so you don't have to do a thing when cooking. Alternatively, there are kebab holders that support the skewers while you do the labor.

ROTISSERIE Rotisserie cooking, or spit-roasting, is a visually entertaining way to barbecue food but it takes a long time. A whole bird, for example, is threaded on a metal spit which is then turned slowly over the fire. Rotisseries can be simple hand-turned varieties or modern battery-operated units which are much more convenient. Apart from turning, little attention is needed during cooking, though you may like to brush with a baste from about halfway through cooking time. Spit-roasting a 3-pound chicken would take 1½ hours.

To speed up cooking time and ensure even cooking, fit reflectors to the sides of the barbecue at the height of the food. And to prevent flare-ups, place a drip tray directly under the meat to catch the fat.

COVERED BARBECUES Barbecues with lids are more like outdoor ovens enabling you to bake, grill and smoke food. You adjust the dampers to increase or reduce the temperature or maintain the required heat.

GOURMET GARDEN DINING

What better way to enjoy a meal than in your own garden? All you need is some comfortable garden furniture and you're set. Make sure you put your table and chairs in the shade for those hot summer days.

Eating in the garden at night in the fresh night air is also a treat — light the table with candles for a pleasing effect.

Once you are all set up, turn to our delicious recipes for garden meals and whip up a feast.

PACKING A PICNIC

These days going on a picnic is easy with the modern day picnic sets that come with all sorts of useful utensils and containers. However, you don't need to rush out and buy a picnic set — most of us have everything we need at home. Of course a picnic basket does come in handy to carry everything to the picnic spot, particularly if it's far from the car! Don't forget to take a blanket, and a plastic bag for rubbish is a good idea.

It's best to take nonbreakable plates, cups and glasses as these can be stacked with no fear of damage. Always rinse if possible before packing back into the hamper at the end of the picnic or it will be a mess by the time you get home.

It's important to take food that is easy to pack, easy to eat and easy to put away to go home, so it may be best to forget anything that's heavy on the sauce. Pack all food in containers that don't leak.

Sandwiches of course are the ever useful, versatile and non-messy picnic food and with some imagination even these can be creative. Tasty pastries, tarts and pies are always good as well as cold meats and munchies like olives and sun dried tomatoes. Take breads and crackers with dips (in tightly sealed containers). Salads are always great to pick at, but keep the dressing in a jar until you are ready to eat. For dessert, cakes may be a pleasure to look at, but slices, muffins and biscuits are easier to pass around. Watch out for the ants.

In the beverage department, wine and beer are always popular and of course, fruit juice, soft drinks and water. Pack ice in a separate bag in the cooler to keep the drinks refreshed.

In our chapter *Portable Picnics* you will find irresistible recipes for a perfect picnic.

SUPER SALADS

The boring garden salad with lettuce, tomato and cucumber is a thing of the past. Salads can be creative, delicious combinations of all sorts of vegetables and other ingredients. They can also be terribly simple — try combining three or four kinds of lettuce with some chopped fresh herbs and a special vinaigrette dressing of your choice. The salads in our chapter *Something on the Side* will give you ideas to create your own and the recipes for dressings and mayonnaises will convert any salad into something special.

All you need for a successful salad are fresh ingredients, and the rest is easy. A perfect meal for a summer's day could be made out of lots of salads with some crusty, hearty breads. So simple and so healthful. See our tables *Salad Greens* and *Salad Vegetables*.

Brilliant Barbecues

Barbecues are a traditional way of cooking food out-of-doors, and while they can be simple and easy, they have also developed into a more formal way of presenting food. Marinades can transform a plain steak into something special and with today's awareness of eating healthily, seafood is enjoying a new lease of life on the barbecue. Yet what could be more relaxing, or enjoyable, than entertaining guests who come and chat to the cook over the coals?

Plate from Pillivuyt, glasses from Orrefors Kosta Boda

Fire Starters

Don't keep your guests starving while the meat's on the barbecue: serve up some of these delicious appetizers, many of which can be prepared in advance. There are spreads, pâtés, curry puffs and meatballs, to name a few.

OYSTER CHEESE PUFFS

½ cup butter

2 cups grated tasty cheese

2½ teaspoons sherry

1 egg, separated

Two 3½-ounce cans smoked oysters, drained

2 loaves French bread, cut into 2-inch rounds

1 tablespoon finely chopped fresh parsley

paprika, to taste

Heat oven to 450°F.

Beat butter, cheese and sherry together. Add egg yolk and beat well. Whisk egg white until soft peaks form. Fold egg white into cheese mixture.

Place 1 oyster onto each round of bread. Top with a teaspoonful of cheese mixture. Sprinkle with chopped parsley and paprika and place on baking sheets. Bake for 10 minutes and serve piping hot.

MAKES 24 TO 32

CHIVE AND PECAN CHEESE ROUNDS

¾ cup ricotta cheese

5 ounces (1½ cups) aged cheddar, finely grated

½ teaspoon freshly ground black pepper

1 tablespoon chopped fresh chives

½ teaspoon cayenne

¾ cup finely chopped pecans

Combine ricotta, cheddar, pepper, chives and cayenne. Cover with plastic wrap and refrigerate until firm. Shape into 2 small rounds and roll in pecans. Serve with small rounds of crusty bread.

SERVES 2 TO 4

CHOPPING CHIVES

An easy way to chop chives is to snip them with sharp scissors. The whole stem can be used.
The flowers make a very attractive garnish.

CHEESE AND PORT SPREAD

6 tablespoons butter, softened

4 ounces creamy blue-veined cheese

4 ounces smoked cheese, finely grated

1 tablespoon port

½ tablespoon white pepper

Beat butter and cheeses until smooth.

Mix through port and pepper.

Spoon into serving dish and chill before serving.

SERVES 8

Roasted Pepper Dip (page 22), Warm Salad of Barbecued Beef and Radicchio (page 37), Pear and Brie Chicken (page 33)

Chive and Pecan Cheese Rounds, Cheese and Port Spread

SALMON AND CHIVE LOG

- 8 ounces cream cheese
- 3 tablespoons sour cream
- 1 tablespoon fresh lemon juice
- 3 scallions, chopped
- 2 bunches chives, finely chopped
- One 14-ounce can red salmon, drained and boned
- 1 teaspoon freshly ground black pepper
- ⅓ cup chopped pecan nuts

Beat cream cheese, sour cream and lemon juice until smooth.

Fold in the scallions, a quarter of the chives, salmon and pecans. Refrigerate until firm.

Place mixture on a sheet of plastic wrap and shape into a log. Roll the cheese log in remaining chives and refrigerate until needed. Serve with crackers or bread.

SERVES 4 TO 6

COCONUT CURRY PUFFS

- 1 tablespoon oil
- 1 onion, chopped
- 2 cloves garlic, crushed
- 1 pound ground beef or lamb
- 1 tablespoon curry paste or powder
- 1 tablespoon chopped coriander
- 1 red chile, chopped
- 1 potato, grated
- 1 cup coconut milk
- 1 package prepared puff pastry (about 2 pounds)
- 1 egg, lightly beaten
- oil for frying

In a large pan, sauté onion, garlic and meat in oil until brown. Add curry paste, coriander, chile, potato and coconut milk.

Simmer for 8 minutes or until mixture is thick. Allow to cool.

Cut pastry into 2½-inch rounds. Place a spoonful of filling onto each round. Brush edges of pastry with egg and press to seal. Deep fry in hot oil until golden.

MAKES 15

SALMON AND LIME PÂTÉ

- Two 14-ounce cans pink salmon, drained and bones removed
- 1 large cucumber, peeled, seeded and chopped
- 2 scallions, chopped
- 3 tablespoons lime juice
- 1 tablespoon grated lime rind
- ½ cup mayonnaise
- 1 tablespoon Dijon mustard
- 1 tablespoon gelatin dissolved in ¼ cup boiling water

Coconut Curry Puffs

Put salmon, cucumber, scallions, lime juice and rind, mayonnaise and mustard in a food processor or blender and process until smooth.

Stir gelatin mixture through salmon mixture. Pour into a lightly oiled mold. Cover and chill for 4 hours or until set.

SERVES 8 TO 10

SPICY SKEWERED MEATBALLS

1 pound lean ground beef

1 onion, finely chopped

1 egg, lightly beaten

1 cup fresh bread crumbs

3 tablespoons tomato sauce

3 tablespoons sweet chili sauce

1 teaspoon ground cumin

1 tablespoon chopped fresh parsley

Spicy Skewered Meatballs

Combine beef, onion, egg, bread crumbs, tomato sauce, chili sauce, cumin and parsley.

Roll mixture into small balls. Place 2 meatballs on each skewer and barbecue or broil, turning frequently for 10 minutes or until cooked. Serve with a spicy dipping sauce.

MAKES 18

BALSAMIC SMOKED BEEF ROUNDS

12 small slices bread

½ cup sour cream

½ teaspoon horseradish

1 teaspoon grainy mustard

12 slices smoked beef

1 tablespoon balsamic vinegar

freshly ground pepper

1 tablespoon small basil leaves

Spread bread slices with combined sour cream, horseradish and mustard.

Top with smoked beef, sprinkle with balsamic vinegar, pepper and basil.

SERVES 6

HERB PANCAKES WITH AVOCADO BUTTER

½ cup all-purpose flour, sifted

½ cup self-rising flour, sifted

1 egg, lightly beaten

½ cup milk

3 to 4 tablespoons chopped fresh mixed herbs

1 teaspoon freshly ground pepper

A V O C A D O   B U T T E R

½ avocado

4 tablespoons butter

1 tablespoon fresh lemon or lime juice

½ teaspoon freshly ground pepper

Place flours, egg, milk, herbs and pepper in a small bowl and whisk until smooth.

Pour spoonfuls of batter onto a hot griddle.

Herb Pancakes with Avocado Butter,
Balsamic Smoked Beef Rounds

Cook until golden brown on both sides. Keep warm.

To Make Avocado Butter: Place avocado, butter, lemon juice and pepper in a small bowl and mix until smooth. Spread on top of pancakes and serve.

SERVES 8 TO 10

MUSHROOM AND HAM PASTRIES

4 sheets of frozen puff pastry, thawed

1 egg, beaten

F I L L I N G

¼ pound ham, diced

1 onion, chopped

¼ pound mushrooms, sliced

2 tablespoons butter

1 celery stalk, chopped

1 tablespoon chopped fresh parsley

1 tablespoon tomato purée or paste

freshly ground black pepper, to taste

Preheat oven to 420°F.

Sauté ham, onion and mushrooms in butter until onion is transparent. Add celery, parsley, tomato purée and pepper. Cook until liquid has evaporated. Remove from heat and cool.

Cut pastry sheets into 9 4-inch rounds. Place a tablespoon of mixture on one half of each round. Fold over pastry to form half moon shape. Press edges together to seal, and use prongs of a fork for decoration. Brush with beaten egg.

Place pastries on baking tray. Bake for 15 to 20 minutes. Serve hot or cold.

MAKES 36

Shrimp with Creamy Cashew Nut Sauce

PREPARING SHRIMP

Cut off the head, remove the tail and shell. Use a sharp knife to devein them. Shrimp are cooked when they're red.

SHRIMP WITH CREAMY CASHEW NUT SAUCE

½ cup finely chopped cashew nuts

1 clove garlic, crushed

3 tablespoons light soy sauce

1 teaspoon grated lemon rind

1 red chile, chopped

½ cup cream

1 tablespoon cornstarch blended with 1 tablespoon water

2 pounds shrimp, shelled and deveined with tails on

Place cashew nuts, garlic, soy, lemon rind, chile, cream and cornstarch mixture in a small pan. Stir over a low heat until mixture thickens.

Thread shrimp onto skewers and barbecue or grill, basting frequently with sauce. Serve with remaining sauce.

SERVES 6 TO 8

SMOKED TROUT TARTLETS

1 loaf sliced white bread

4 tablespoons butter, melted

FILLING

1 smoked trout (about ¾ pound), skinned and boned

¼ cup mayonnaise

2 scallions, finely chopped

1 tablespoon chopped chives

1 teaspoon horseradish cream

1 teaspoon mustard

1 teaspoon freshly ground black pepper

black olives, pitted and cut into strips

Preheat oven to 200°F.

Trim crusts from bread and flatten with a rolling pin. Brush both sides with butter and press into tartlet tins. Bake for 10 minutes or until crisp and golden. Cool.

To Prepare Filling: In a small bowl break trout into small pieces with a fork. Add mayonnaise, scallions, chives, horseradish, mustard and pepper and mix well.

Spoon trout filling into tart cases, garnish with strips of olives and serve immediately.

MAKES 34

KEBABS

Flat, metal skewers with an insulated handle are best for kebabs on the barbecue. If you are using bamboo satay sticks, soak them in water beforehand. You could also make some hairpin style skewers. Bend stainless steel wire into hairpin-shaped skewers about 8 inches long and ½ inch wide.

CHEESE AND OLIVE MELTS

These are great to make while the barbecue is heating up to its full potential.

12 slices olive bread

⅔ cup grated smoked cheese

⅔ cup grated Swiss cheese

½ cup chopped olives

1 tablespoon thyme leaves

Place 2 slices of olive bread on a piece of foil. Top with smoked cheese, Swiss cheese, olives and thyme. Seal foil package. Repeat with remaining ingredients.

Place on a warm barbecue and cook for 4 to 5 minutes or until cheese is warm and melted. These can also be cooked under a hot broiler until golden and cheese is bubbling.

SERVES 6

Smoked Trout Tartlets

PEPPERED CHICKEN PÂTÉ

- *1 pound chicken livers, trimmed*
- *1 onion, chopped*
- *2 cloves garlic, crushed*
- *½ pound (2 sticks) unsalted butter*
- *1 tablespoon chopped fresh sage*
- *3 tablespoons chopped fresh basil*
- *1 tablespoon freshly ground black pepper*
- *3 tablespoons brandy*
- *fresh bay leaves (if unavailable, use dried)*
- *6 tablespoons clarified butter, melted*

Roughly chop livers and add to a hot pan with onion, garlic and 4 tablespoons of the butter. Sauté this mixture until livers are lightly cooked and onion is soft.

Place liver mixture, herbs (except for bay leaves), remaining butter, pepper and brandy into a food processor or blender and process until smooth.

Pour mixture into a terrine or serving dish and chill until slightly set. Arrange bay leaves on top of pâté. Pour over clarified butter and chill until firm.

SERVES 6 TO 8

CLARIFIED BUTTER

Clarified butter, also called ghee, is butter fat with the milk solids and salt removed. It can be heated to greater temperatures than fresh butter without burning and is therefore often used for frying, especially in Indian cooking. It also imparts a different flavor and color to fresh butter. Ghee is sold in cans or jars in Indian groceries and will keep refrigerated for many months, or even unrefrigerated for many weeks in cool surroundings. You can make your own clarified butter by heating fresh butter gently until a foam forms on the top. Cook a few seconds more then remove from heat. A milky residue will sink to the bottom, leaving the clear clarified butter on the top. Pour this into another container.

BARBECUE BRUSCHETTA

These can be made while standing around the barbecue, or on the stove inside. Either way these simple munchies are very easy and a definite crowd pleaser.

BASIC BRUSCHETTA

- *12 small slices of crusty bread*
- *3 tablespoons olive oil*
- *2 cloves garlic, halved*

Brush both sides of bread with olive oil. Place on barbecue or under broiler until both sides are golden brown.

Rub toasted bread with garlic and serve plain or with any of the following toppings.

SERVES 6 TO 12

TOMATO, SAGE AND RED ONION

- *2 tomatoes, chopped*
- *1 tablespoon chopped sage leaves*
- *1 red onion, finely sliced*
- *1 teaspoon freshly ground pepper*

Cook tomato, sage, red onion and pepper on griddle or in a pan and toss until mixture is hot.

MUSHROOM AND PEPPER

- *½ pound small button mushrooms, halved*
- *½ red pepper, chopped*
- *½ yellow pepper, chopped*
- *3 tablespoons chopped fresh basil*
- *freshly ground pepper*

Sauté mushrooms, peppers, basil and a few grindings of pepper on the barbecue griddle or in a pan for 3 to 4 minutes.

ZUCCHINI AND FETA

- *2 zucchini, thinly sliced*
- *6 sun dried tomatoes, chopped*
- *½ pound feta cheese, crumbled*

Place zucchini, tomatoes and feta on a barbecue griddle or in a pan. Cook for 3 to 4 minutes or until heated through.

Peppered Chicken Pâté

MEDITERRANEAN OYSTERS

24 oysters in the shell

¼ cup balsamic vinegar

6 slices prosciutto, chopped

freshly ground pepper

Preheat broiler.

Sprinkle oysters with balsamic vinegar. Top with pieces of prosciutto and pepper.

Place under broiler for 1 minute or until prosciutto is crisp.

SERVES 4 TO 6

HONEYED SHRIMP

2 pounds cooked large shrimp, shelled and deveined

MARINADE

1 cup dark honey

1 cup tomato sauce

½ cup olive oil

freshly ground black pepper

1 tablespoon dry mustard

dash of hot pepper sauce

Combine marinade ingredients in a bowl and blend well. Marinate shrimp 15 to 30 minutes then thread 2 to 3 shrimp on each skewer and barbecue over a good hot fire. Brush with remaining marinade and turn. Barbecue time about 5 to 6 minutes.

SERVES 6 TO 8

CHAR-GRILLED BABY OCTOPUS WITH PESTO MAYONNAISE

2 pounds baby octopus, cleaned and halved

1 clove garlic, crushed

3 tablespoons brown sugar

½ cup red wine

1 tablespoon lemon thyme leaves

PESTO MAYONNAISE

½ cup mayonnaise

½ cup prepared pesto

Place octopus, garlic, sugar, wine and thyme in a bowl and marinate for 1 to 2 hours.

Cook on a hot griddle, turning regularly until octopus is cooked and tender.

To Make Pesto Mayonnaise: Mix mayonnaise and pesto. Serve with octopus as a dip or spoon over as a sauce.

SERVES 8 TO 10

MARINADE FOR OCTOPUS

A very simple way to barbecue octopus is to marinate it in a mixture of olive oil, fresh lemon juice, crushed garlic and fresh parsley. After cleaning the octopus, brush with marinade and barbecue for 10 minutes. The octopus will curl and then turn a claret red color which looks very attractive in a garlic salad. If octopus is tough, tenderize before cooking by steaming for about 4 to 5 minutes.

Mediterranean Oysters, Char-grilled Baby Octopus with Pesto Mayonnaise

ROASTED PEPPER DIP

3 red peppers

3 tablespoons tomato paste

2 scallions, chopped

1 tablespoon chopped basil

1 tablespoon balsamic vinegar

1 package (5–6 ounces) cream cheese

1 teaspoon freshly ground pepper

Preheat broiler.

Halve peppers and remove seeds. Flatten slightly. Place under broiler and cook until skins are charred and black. Place peppers in a plastic bag to sweat for 5 minutes. Peel away charred skins.

Dice two-thirds of the roasted peppers and place in a bowl with tomato paste, scallions, basil, and balsamic vinegar.

Put the remaining peppers and the cream cheese in a blender or food processor and process until smooth. Fold into tomato mixture and season with pepper to taste. Serve chilled as a spread or as a dip for crudités.

SERVES 4 TO 6

SESAME DRUMSTICKS

8 chicken legs

¼ cup seasoned flour

1 egg, lightly beaten

¼ cup milk

¼ cup sesame seeds

¼ cup fresh bread crumbs

4 tablespoons butter, melted

Preheat oven to 350°F.

Dust chicken lightly in flour. Dip into combined egg and milk. Roll in combined sesame seeds and bread crumbs.

Place chicken legs in a greased baking dish and bake for 30 minutes.

Brush chicken with butter, return to oven, and bake for a further 15 minutes or until cooked. Serve hot or cold.

SERVES 6 TO 8

Sesame Drumsticks

MARINATED BOCCONCINI

½ cup olive oil

sprigs of fresh herbs (thyme, dill, basil, tarragon)

1 tablespoon freshly ground pepper

6 to 8 bocconcini

Place oil, herbs and pepper in a small saucepan and heat until oil is warm. Keep oil at a low temperature for 5 minutes.

Remove pan from heat and allow to cool completely.

Place bocconcini in a clean glass jar. Pour over oil, seal and place in the refrigerator. Allow to stand for 2 days before serving.

SERVES 6 TO 8

Marinated Bocconcini

BOCCONCINI

'Bocconcini' means 'little mouthfuls'. They are little balls of cheese, usually mozarella. Bocconcini should only be bought when required. They can be stored in a cold refrigerator for up to 3 weeks but will ripen and become firm and dry. Do not use if they turn yellow.

Serving with Sizzle

Barbecuing can be far more tantalizing than steak and sausages. Here are a variety of recipes for beef, lamb, chicken, fish, lobster and shellfish to serve as the main course at a barbecue. Many of these involve marinades so make sure you prepare them in plenty of time for the barbecue.

CHAR-GRILLED BEEF WITH AVOCADO AND TOMATOES

4 steaks (fillet or rump)

2 cloves garlic, crushed

1 tablespoon freshly ground pepper

1 avocado, sliced

8 sun dried tomatoes, sliced

1 tablespoon chopped basil

Trim steaks of any visible fat or sinew, and sprinkle with garlic and pepper.

Place steaks on a hot grill and cook for 3 to 4 minutes.

Turn and top the cooked side with avocado slices, tomatoes and basil. The topping will become warm while the other side is cooking.

Finish cooking steaks to your liking and serve with a mixed lettuce salad.

SERVES 4

GREEK BROCHETTES

1 pound lean lamb, cut in 1½-inch cubes

1½ cups pitted black olives

½ pound goat or feta cheese, cubed

1 pint cherry tomatoes

3 tablespoons olive oil

3 tablespoons chopped fresh thyme

1 tablespoon grated lemon rind

1 tablespoon freshly ground pepper

Thread lamb, olives, cheese and cherry tomatoes onto metal skewers.

Combine the oil, thyme, lemon and pepper.

Brush thyme baste over brochettes and barbecue until tender, turning and basting frequently.

SERVES 4

EASY FOOD PREPARATION

Try to prepare as much food as possible in advance. Choose foods that can remain in the refrigerator or freezer for a few days, so that once the guests arrive, only the barbecue items are left to cook.

Char-grilled Beef with Avocado and Tomatoes, Greek Brochettes

SPICY FISH KEBABS

*2 pounds firm white fish fillets
(bass, shark, swordfish)*

MARINADE

2 cloves garlic, crushed

⅔ cup plain yogurt

1 teaspoon chopped fresh ginger

1 red chile, finely chopped

1 tablespoon garam masala

*1 tablespoon chopped fresh
coriander*

Cut fish fillets into 1-inch cubes.

To Make Marinade: Combine garlic,
yogurt, ginger, chile, garam masala
and coriander.

Thread fish cubes onto skewers.
Pour marinade over fish and
refrigerate for 1 hour.

Grill or barbecue skewers for 5 to
6 minutes. Serve with flat bread and
salad.

SERVES 6

HONEY LAMB SKEWERS

*2 pounds lean lamb, cut into
½-inch cubes*

2 onions, cut into small wedges

MARINADE

¼ cup dry white wine

2 tablespoons hoisin sauce

3 tablespoons sherry

3 tablespoons honey

1 clove garlic, crushed

To Make Marinade: Combine wine,
hoisin, sherry, honey and garlic. Mix
thoroughly with the lamb and
refrigerate for 2 hours.

Thread pieces of lamb and onions
onto skewers. Grill or barbecue for
6 to 8 minutes and serve with a
crisp salad.

SERVES 6

BUYING MEAT

Cheaper cuts don't suddenly become top
quality on the barbecue. Buy good meat.
Don't spoil the good feeling that you get
from the great outdoors with cheap meat.
Good meat is good value. There's no
waste because it's all eaten. The flesh
should have good texture, and the fat
should be firm and white.

SHRIMP WITH LIME AND CORIANDER BUTTER

2 pounds large shrimp

3 cloves garlic

3 tablespoons oil

**LIME AND
CORIANDER BUTTER**

6 tablespoons butter

1 tablespoon grated lime rind

3 tablespoons lime juice

¼ cup chopped coriander

1 teaspoon freshly ground pepper

To Make Lime and Coriander Butter:
Combine butter, lime rind and juice,
coriander and pepper. Place mixture
on a piece of plastic wrap and roll
into a log. Refrigerate until solid.

Put shrimp, garlic and oil on a hot
barbecue griddle and toss for 3 to
4 minutes or until hot and shrimp
change color. Cut butter into rounds
and serve with hot shrimp.

SERVES 4 TO 6

ITALIAN FISH IN FOIL

One 2-pound whole fish, cleaned and scaled (whiting, bream, snapper)

⅓ cup fresh lemon juice

2 onions, sliced into rings

½ pound mushrooms, sliced

4 tomatoes, sliced

pepper to taste

5 tablespoons butter

3 tablespoons lemon zest, julienned

Rinse fish thoroughly and pat with paper towels. Place on foil, sprinkle with lemon juice, and cover with onion rings, mushrooms, tomatoes and pepper. Dot with butter and top with lemon zest. Cover and seal fish with a second piece of foil to make a package.

Barbecue over hot coals for 25 to 35 minutes. Serve fish with the vegetables and the juices in the foil.

SERVES 4 TO 6

SHRIMP WITH CREAMY SATAY SAUCE

1 clove garlic, crushed

½ cup crunchy peanut butter

3 tablespoons soy sauce

3 tablespoons fresh lemon juice

1 tablespoon grated lemon rind

¼ cup water

1 red chile, seeded and finely chopped

½ cup cream

2 pounds shrimp, shelled and deveined with tails left intact

Mix garlic, peanut butter, soy, lemon juice and rind, water and chile in a small saucepan, and stir over low heat until sauce simmers and thickens. Stir in cream.

Thread shrimp onto bamboo skewers and brush with satay sauce.

Cook shrimp on grill or under a broiler for 4 to 5 minutes basting with satay sauce.

Serve hot with remaining satay sauce.

SERVES 8 TO 10

TIPS FOR BARBECUING SEAFOOD

Don't barbecue seafood over a flaming fire. Wait till the fire dies down to glowing embers. If using a griddle this is not necessary, but grease the griddle well. If using an electric barbecue, make sure the grill is well greased. Gas barbecuing is an ideal way to barbecue seafood as you have control over the temperature. Again, make sure the grill is greased. Fish can be barbecued whole, filleted or as steaks. Score larger fish — that is, cut through the flesh a few times to the bone on both sides, so that heat can penetrate.

CONTROL THE HEAT

Flame does not cook meat, it burns fat. Control the heat by damping charcoal. For gas or electric barbecues, lower the flame or thermostat, or move the food off the direct heat, to control the cooking. When damping, sprinkle water carefully, just to reduce the temperature. Don't overdo it. If your grill is very close to the coals, move food to one side while you damp down.

TANDOORI CHICKEN

16 chicken pieces, skinned

MARINADE

2 onions, grated

3 cloves garlic, crushed

4 tablespoons fresh lemon juice

TANDOORI PASTE

1½ cups yogurt

1 tablespoon ground coriander

1 tablespoon ground cumin

1 tablespoon turmeric

1 teaspoon ground cayenne

red food coloring (optional)

Prick chicken pieces with a fork.

To Make Marinade: Mix the onions, garlic and lemon juice and pour over chicken pieces. Let stand 30 minutes.

To Make Tandoori Paste: Combine yogurt, coriander, cumin, turmeric, cayenne and food coloring. Pour over chicken and toss to coat evenly. Cover and refrigerate for 12 hours or overnight.

Cook chicken over glowing coals for 20 to 30 minutes or until cooked.

SERVES 8

Tandoori Chicken, Shrimp with Creamy Satay Sauce

MINTED LAMB BURGERS

MINTED BUTTER

¼ pound (1 stick) butter, softened

¼ cup chopped fresh mint

BURGERS

2 pounds ground lamb

1 onion, finely chopped

2 cloves garlic, crushed

3 tablespoons chopped fresh mint

1 teaspoon paprika

1 egg, lightly beaten

To Make Minted Butter: Mix butter and mint. Place on a sheet of plastic wrap and roll into a log shape. Chill until firm.

To Make Burgers: Mix the lamb, onion, garlic, mint, paprika and egg.

Shape mixture into 6 patties. Barbecue over hot coals for 5 to 8 minutes or until cooked.

Serve on rolls or buns and top with rounds of minted butter, and with a salad of your choice.

SERVES 6

Minted Lamb Burgers

GLAZED SIRLOINS

2 sirloin steaks, cut into
6 serving pieces

MARINADE

¼ cup soy sauce

¼ cup dry sherry

1 tablespoon Worcestershire sauce

2 cloves garlic, crushed

1 tablespoon white vinegar

3 tablespoons brown sugar

Trim steaks of any excess fat and place in a shallow container.

To Make Marinade: Combine soy sauce, sherry, Worcestershire sauce, garlic, vinegar and sugar. Pour over steaks and refrigerate for 2 to 3 hours.

To cook, remove steaks from marinade and broil on a hot grill 4 to 5 minutes each side. Brush with remaining marinade while cooking.

SERVES 6

RARE, MEDIUM OR WELL-DONE?

No two guests like their steak quite the same. How can you serve everyone hot food at the same time and still be able to tell which steaks are rare and which are well-done? Like so many things, it is easy once you know how. Cut your steaks to different thicknesses. Thick for rare, a little thinner for medium and so on. The bonus is that all are ready at the same time and you can easily tell, by the thickness, which is which. Serve more of the thinner ones of course!

BARBECUED FILLET WITH HORSERADISH CREAM

3 pound fillet of beef

6 slices bacon

MARINADE

1 onion, roughly chopped

1 cup port

4 peppercorns

1 clove garlic, crushed

HORSERADISH CREAM

1 cup thickened cream, whipped

1 tablespoon horseradish

1 scallion, finely sliced

1 tablespoon chopped fresh parsley

Remove any visible fat or sinew from meat. Wrap bacon around fillet in a spiral fashion and secure with toothpicks.

To Make Marinade: Place onion, port, peppercorns and garlic in a large plastic bag. Place fillet in bag and toss well to coat. Seal bag and refrigerate for 3 to 4 hours, turning bag occasionally. Remove fillet from marinade and barbecue until meat is cooked to your liking.

To Make Horseradish Cream: Fold together cream, horseradish, scallion and parsley.

To serve, cut fillet into very thin slices and serve with horseradish cream.

SERVES 8

LEMON AND PEPPER COD

Any fish steak can be used in this recipe.

6 cod steaks

2 lemons, thinly sliced

3 tablespoons chopped fresh dill

2 tablespoons green peppercorns

½ cup dry white wine

dill, to garnish

Place cod steaks on 6 individual pieces of foil. Top each with lemon slices, dill and peppercorns.

Bring edges of foil together to form an open package. Sprinkle a small amount of wine over each steak and seal foil edges together.

Barbecue the packages for 8 to 10 minutes and serve with extra dill.

SERVES 6

Glazed Sirloins, Lemon and Pepper Cod

BARBECUED OREGANO CHICKEN

2 pounds chicken pieces

1 tablespoon salt

MARINADE

½ cup fresh lemon juice

1 tablespoon grated lemon rind

½ cup olive oil

1 tablespoon freshly ground pepper

¼ cup roughly chopped fresh oregano

Rub chicken pieces with salt, place in a bowl and allow to stand 5 minutes.

To Make Marinade: Mix the lemon juice, rind, oil, pepper and oregano. Pour over chicken pieces, cover with plastic wrap and refrigerate overnight.

Cook chicken pieces on barbecue basting frequently with marinade until cooked.

SERVES 4

CAJUN BLACKENED CHICKEN

6 skinless and boneless chicken breasts

6 tablespoons butter, melted

CAJUN SPICE

2 cloves garlic, crushed

1 small onion, grated

1 tablespoon freshly ground pepper

1 tablespoon cayenne

1 tablespoon paprika

Brush both sides of chicken with butter.

To Make Cajun Spice: Combine the garlic, onion, pepper, cayenne and paprika. Rub generously into chicken.

Barbecue on a smoking griddle until outside of chicken is black and inside is tender.

SERVES 6

Barbecued Oregano Chicken

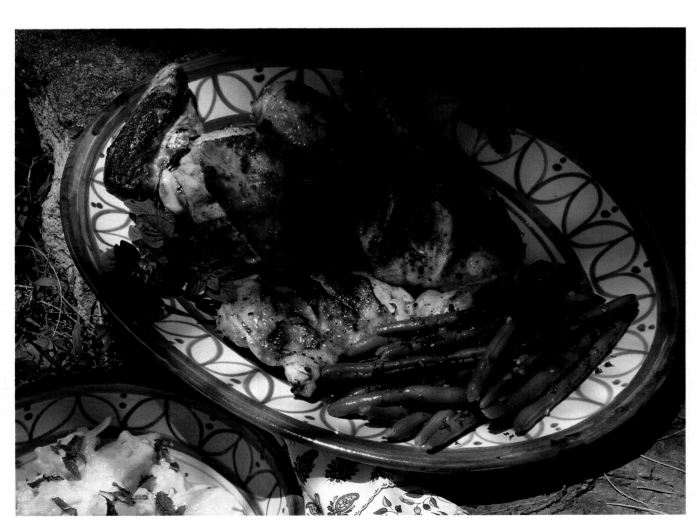

PEAR AND BRIE CHICKEN

6 skinless and boneless chicken breasts

3 tablespoons lime juice

1 tablespoon sea salt

2 pears, peeled and chopped

4 tablespoons butter

½ pound Brie, sliced

Rub chicken with lime juice and salt. Place on a hot barbecue plate with pears and butter. Cook chicken and pears until golden brown on both sides.

Place Brie slices over chicken and allow to melt slightly. Remove from barbecue and serve chicken with the golden pears.

SERVES 6

Pear and Brie Chicken

RED MULLET IN CORN HUSKS

*6 small red mullet, cleaned and
scaled*

12 sprigs lemon thyme

1 lemon, sliced

2 cloves garlic, sliced

6 large fresh corn husks

olive oil

freshly ground pepper

Fill cavity of fish with thyme, lemon
and garlic.

Place each fish on a corn husk.
Sprinkle with oil and pepper. Tie
each end to the husks with string.

Place directly on coals or on grill
and cook for 5 to 6 minutes or until
fish is cooked.

SERVES 6

CLEANING BARBECUES

A barbecue is much easier to clean when
it is warm rather than when it is cold.
Clean your barbecue after using it, or heat
the grill before use and clean it.

CHAR-GRILLED SCALLOPS WITH LIME HOLLANDAISE

1 pound scallops

3 tablespoons olive oil

*1 tablespoon freshly ground
pepper*

LIME HOLLANDAISE

6 ounces (1½ sticks) butter

¼ cup water

3 egg yolks

1 tablespoon fresh lime juice

1 tablespoon grated lime rind

Thread scallops onto skewers.
Sprinkle with oil and sprinkle with
pepper.

To Make Lime Hollandaise: Melt
butter in a small saucepan and allow
to cool. Whisk together the water
and egg yolks in a bowl. Place bowl
over a pan of simmering water and
beat until egg mixture is thick (about
3 minutes). Remove bowl from heat
and slowly whisk in the butter. Stir
through lime juice and rind.

Char-grill scallops on a hot barbecue,
and serve, topped with Lime
Hollandaise.

SERVES 4 TO 6

*Red Mullet in Corn Husks, Char-grilled
Scallops with Lime Hollandaise*

CHICKEN WITH SPICY PECAN STUFFING

4 skinless and boneless chicken breasts

SPICY PECAN STUFFING

½ pound cream cheese, softened

1 teaspoon ground cumin

1 teaspoon ground coriander

1 teaspoon cayenne

¾ cup chopped pecans

Pound chicken between two sheets of plastic wrap or wax paper until thin.

To Make Stuffing: Combine cream cheese, cumin, coriander, cayenne and pecan nuts.

Place stuffing down the center of each chicken fillet. Roll to enclose stuffing and secure with toothpicks.

Grill for 6 minutes or until tender. Slice and serve.

SERVES 4

BARBECUING POULTRY

Poultry has long been popular at barbecues with both cooks and guests. It's a flexible ingredient and a convenient finger food. Whole chickens can be spit-roasted in 1 to 1½ hours, chicken pieces basted and barbecued and fillets from the breast or thigh cut into bite-sized chunks and served as kebabs or satés. Always buy good quality chicken, turkey or duck and cook same-sized pieces so that you can serve everyone hot food at the same time.

PIQUANT FISH STEAKS

4 fish steaks (tuna, salmon or halibut)

MARINADE

10 fresh bay leaves (if unavailable, use dried)

4 cardamom pods

¼ cup olive oil

1 tablespoon coriander seeds

3 tablespoons chopped chives

2 limes, sliced

1 tablespoon freshly ground pepper

Place fish in a large shallow dish.

To Make Marinade: Bruise the (fresh) bay leaves and cardamom, and mix with the oil, coriander, chives, lime and pepper. Pour marinade over fish. Cover and refrigerate for 3 to 4 hours, turning fish once.

Remove fish and barbecue until tender, brushing with marinade while cooking. Serve with a squeeze of lime or lemon.

SERVES 4

CHILI BARBECUE SPARERIBS

3 pounds spareribs

MARINADE

1 cup tomato purée

3 tablespoons chili sauce

3 tablespoons Worcestershire sauce

2 cloves garlic, crushed

3 tablespoons brown sugar

few drops hot pepper sauce

Trim ribs of any excess fat. Cut racks into single ribs. Place ribs in a large shallow dish.

To Make Marinade: Place tomato purée, chili sauce, Worcestershire sauce, garlic, brown sugar and hot pepper sauce in a small bowl and mix to combine. Pour marinade over ribs, cover and refrigerate for 1 hour.

Cook ribs on a hot grill until tender, brushing with marinade while cooking.

SERVES 4 TO 6

SALT BAKED FISH

2 medium-sized fish (trout, sea bass or snapper), cleaned and scaled

4 sprigs dill

4 cloves garlic, halved

4 pieces lemon rind

10 peppercorns

salt

Fill cavity of fish with dill, garlic, lemon rind and peppercorns.

Place 2 pieces of foil on a board and pour a generous pile of salt down the middle of each piece of foil. Place fish on salt, cover with extra salt. Gather ends of foil and seal.

Place the packages on hot coals and cook for 15 to 20 minutes. Remove fish from foil and scrap away salt. Serve with salad.

SERVES 4 TO 6

WATCHING CALORIES

Barbecuing and spit-roasting meat are two of the least fattening ways of cooking meat. If you are watching your weight, buy lean cuts of meat and trim off the fat before cooking to reduce your cholesterol intake.

WARM SALAD OF BARBECUED BEEF AND RADICCHIO

1 pound fillet steak

1 tablespoon oil

3 tablespoons light soy sauce

3 tablespoons fresh lemon juice

2 red chiles, seeded and chopped

2 cloves garlic, crushed

1 tablespoon shredded ginger

4 tablespoons red wine

2 heads radicchio, roughly torn into pieces

Slice fillet into thin pieces and marinate with oil, soy, lemon juice, chile, garlic, ginger and wine. Cover and refrigerate for 30 minutes.

Toss fillet steak, marinade and radicchio on a hot griddle until tender. Serve warm.

SERVES 4

Warm Salad of Barbecued Beef and Radicchio

BEEF

Best quality beef is unsurpassed on its own or served with horseradish, mustards, savory butters and sauces. Marinating also adds zest to a beef kebab or steak.

PORK AND NECTARINE ROLLS

4 pork cutlets or boneless chops

NECTARINE FILLING

2 nectarines, peeled and sliced

1 cup fresh bread crumbs

3 tablespoons honey

1 tablespoon chopped sage

4 scallions, chopped

honey for glazing

Pound pork between sheets of plastic wrap or wax paper until thin.

To Make Filling: Combine nectarines, bread crumbs, honey, sage and onions.

Place filling down the center of the cutlets. Roll pork over filling and tie with string.

Brush pork with extra honey and cook on barbecue for 10 minutes or until pork is tender. Slice and serve.

SERVES 4

BARBECUED PORK

Well done but not overdone is the rule for pork, so patience and care are required. Keep bastes and sauces free of fat because pork is such a rich meat. It goes well marinated in fruit flavors such as apricot or plum. Buy the best pork. Ask your butcher for cuts without excess bone or fat. To cook crackling without overcooking the meat, take the rind off the meat and cook the skin separately. For crispy, crunchy crackling, rub the skin with oil and salt and cook over medium-to-hot coals.

CHILE PEPPER SHRIMP

12 large shrimp

MARINADE

2 red chiles, seeded and chopped

½ cup tomato purée

2 cloves garlic, crushed

6 scallions, thinly sliced

3 tablespoons chopped fresh basil

3 teaspoons freshly ground pepper

Make a small slit on the underside of each tail to allow marinade to soak through.

To Make Marinade: Combine the chile, tomato, garlic, onions, basil and pepper. Add shrimp, cover and refrigerate for 1 hour.

Cook shrimp with marinade on a hot griddle for 10 to 15 minutes or until flesh is tender. Serve with a leafy salad.

SERVES 6

LOBSTER TAILS WITH MACADAMIAS

2 lobster tails

MARINADE

¼ cup macadamia nut oil (or walnut oil)

3 tablespoons lemon thyme leaves

1 tablespoon grated lime rind

½ cup chopped unsalted macadamia nuts

fresh ground pepper to taste

Cut lobster tails in half lengthwise.

To Make Marinade: Combine oil, thyme, rind and pepper. Brush marinade over lobster flesh, cover, and refrigerate for 1 hour.

Cook on grill flesh side down and brush with marinade until lobster is tender. Warm the macadamia nuts on a griddle or in a skillet and serve on top of lobster.

SERVES 4

TANDOORI LAMB CUTLETS

12 boneless lamb chops

MARINADE

1 cup plain yogurt

4 tablespoons chopped coriander leaves

1 tablespoon ground cumin

2 cloves garlic, crushed

1 tablespoon grated ginger

½ teaspoon turmeric

1 red chile, seeded and finely chopped

To Make Marinade: Combine yogurt, coriander, cumin, garlic, ginger, turmeric and chile. Pour over lamb chops, cover and refrigerate overnight.

Coat chops thickly in tandoori marinade and barbecue on a hot grill until tender. Serve with mint and salad.

SERVES 4

Lobster with Cress and Balsamic Vinegar

GOOD QUALITY MEAT

The golden rule is that good meat doesn't need to be tenderized. It is tender. Marinades offer extra flavors which broaden the barbecue repertoire in the same way as savory butters and delicious sauces for dipping or pouring.

LOBSTER WITH CRESS AND BALSAMIC VINEGAR

2 lobster tails

MARINADE

¼ cup balsamic vinegar

3 tablespoons brown sugar

3 tablespoons dry white wine

⅓ cup chopped watercress

1 tablespoon shredded lemon zest

Remove lobster flesh from shells and slice into thick medallions. Place in a shallow dish.

To Make Marinade: Combine vinegar, sugar, wine, cress and lemon zest. Pour over lobster, cover, and refrigerate for 30 minutes.

Barbecue lobster, brushing with marinade, until tender.

SERVES 4 TO 6

THAI CHICKEN WITH POTATO PANCAKES

6 chicken thighs, skinned and boned

4 tablespoons chopped coriander

2 stalks lemon grass, chopped

1 tablespoon chopped ginger

1 clove garlic, crushed

¼ cup sweet chili sauce

POTATO PANCAKES

6 potatoes, grated

2 eggs, lightly beaten

¼ cup plain flour

3 tablespoons poppy seeds

Trim any excess fat from chicken and cut each thigh in half. Place in a shallow dish with coriander, lemon grass, ginger, garlic and chili sauce. Cover and refrigerate for at least 2 hours.

Barbecue on a hot grill until tender.

To Make Potato Pancakes: Mix the potatoes, eggs, flour and poppy seeds. Fry heaping spoonfuls of mixture on a greased griddle until golden brown on both sides.

To serve, place a small stack of pancakes on each plate and top with chicken pieces.

SERVES 6

PROSCIUTTO WRAPPED PORK FILLETS

4 small pork fillets

1 tablespoon dried marjoram

1 tablespoon freshly ground black pepper

2 cloves garlic, crushed

8 slices prosciutto

Trim any visible fat or sinew from fillets. Combine marjoram, pepper and garlic and roll fillets in this mixture.

Wrap prosciutto around fillets and secure with toothpicks. Cook on barbecue until tender. Serve sliced with fresh fruits.

SERVES 4 TO 6

VEAL WITH SWEET POTATO ROUNDS

6 veal steaks

MARINADE

½ cup dry white wine

6 peppercorns

6 bay leaves

3 tablespoons chopped sage

1 large sweet potato, sliced

3 tablespoons honey

Combine veal, wine, peppercorns, bay leaves and sage in a shallow dish. Let combination stand for 1 hour.

Brush both sides of potato slices with honey.

Place sweet potato rounds on a well-greased grill. Place veal on grill and brush with marinade. Cook until veal and potatoes are tender.

SERVES 6

CRISPY SHRIMP WITH MANGO SALSA

These shrimp can be eaten with their crispy shells or peeled.

2 pounds medium shrimp (about 50 shrimp)

2 cloves garlic, crushed

3 tablespoons finely sliced lemon zest

2 red chiles, seeded and chopped

1 tablespoon ground cumin

3 tablespoons olive oil

3 tablespoons chopped fresh coriander

MANGO SALSA

1 mango, peeled and chopped

2 tablespoons chopped fresh mint

1 teaspoon freshly ground pepper

1 tablespoon honey

Combine the shrimp, garlic, lemon zest, chile, cumin, oil and coriander. Cover and let stand for 1 hour.

Place shrimp and marinade on a hot griddle and cook until crisp.

To Make Salsa: Mix the mango, mint, pepper and honey. Refrigerate until ready to serve.

Serve shrimp with mango salsa.

SERVES 6

Crispy Shrimp with Mango Salsa, Thai Chicken with Potato Pancakes

SPICY BARBECUED LAMB LEG

1 leg of lamb, boned and
   butterflied to net about
   4 pounds

MARINADE

4 tablespoons chopped fresh
   coriander

1 tablespoon black mustard seeds

¼ cup fresh lemon juice

¼ cup soy sauce

¼ cup sweet chili sauce

Trim excess fat and sinew from lamb, and with the point of a knife make small cuts or jabs into the flesh. This will help the marinade seep into the meat. Put the lamb into a large shallow dish.

To Make Marinade: Combine the coriander, mustard seeds, lemon juice, soy and chili sauces and rub into lamb. Cover and refrigerate overnight.

Barbecue over hot coals until lamb is tender – about 25 minutes. Brush frequently while cooking. Serve sliced with flat bread and salad.

SERVES 6 TO 8

SALMON WITH COCONUT CORIANDER SALSA

Note: As the salsa may be served either cool or warm, you should prepare it before grilling the fish.

6 salmon steaks

4 tablespoons butter

¼ cup fresh lemon juice

COCONUT CORIANDER SALSA

1 cup desiccated coconut

¼ cup water

2 green chiles, seeded and chopped

1 tablespoon oil

1 teaspoon black mustard seeds

¼ cup chopped fresh coriander

Wash and dry salmon. Place butter and lemon juice on a hot griddle and heat until foaming. Cook salmon until tender.

To Make Salsa: Place coconut, water and chiles in a food processor or blender and process until smooth. Heat oil in a small pan, add mustard seeds and cook until they pop. Add coconut mixture, cook an additional 3 minutes, and stir through coriander.

Serve salmon with warm or cold salsa.

SERVES 6

MOROCCAN LAMB MEDALLIONS

6 boneless lamb chops or
   medallions

3 tablespoons tomato paste

1 tablespoon ground cinnamon

1 red onion, finely grated

¼ cup chopped fresh parsley

2 red chiles, seeded and chopped

Trim lamb of any fat or sinew. Place in a large shallow dish with tomato paste, cinnamon, onion, parsley and chile. Cover and let stand for at least 2 hours.

Barbecue on a hot grill until tender. Serve with a citrus-based salad and bread.

SERVES 6

Salmon with Coconut Coriander Salsa

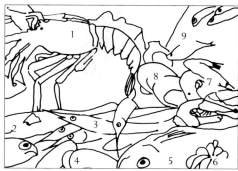

Seafood Selection

1 Lobster 2 Red mullet 3 Garfish
4 New Zealand mussels 5 Snapper
6 Baby octopus 7 Shrimp 8 Scallops
9 Sardines

COOKING FISH

Fish fillets and steaks are delicious
barbecued. They can be cooked on the
barbecue grill, or in foil over a medium
to hot fire. If you are grilling over
charcoal, damp the fire occasionally to
replace lost moisture.

Don't overcook fish. It just becomes
dried out and tasteless. Properly cooked
fish is moist, tender and full of flavor.
It is ready to eat when the flesh is just
starting to flake.

Cooking time depends on thickness. Allow
about 4 to 5 minutes a side for 1-inch-
thick fish cutlets. Turn carefully to
cook other side. Brush with sauce or baste
just before end of cooking time and serve
hot. Marinating adds extra flavor to
seafood. Popular marinade ingredients
include lemon juice, white wine, oil, finely-
diced scallions, soy or teriyaki
sauces, fresh ginger and fresh herbs to
taste. Marinades can also be used for
basting during cooking.

Breads and Spreads

A selection of interesting and tasty breads transforms a barbecue into something special. Filled breads can almost form a meal in themselves! Prepare them before the guests arrive and then bake them either in the coals or in the oven so that you have something to serve immediately. The spreads below will transform the plainest bread into a treat.

SAVORY BUTTERS

Savory butters with herbs and spices can be made in advance and stored in the refrigerator. Mix butter and herbs, roll in wax paper into a log shape, then wrap tightly in freezer paper and foil. Store in the freezer and slice as needed. Savory butters are great with sizzling steaks and vegetables. Try some of these suggestions:

• Cream butter with finely mashed anchovy fillets. Use with fish and veal.

• Pound fresh basil in a mortar and pestle and cream into butter. Delicious with vegetable, rice or pasta.

• Beat butter with Dijon mustard and horseradish. Excellent with meat or fish.

• Cream butter with either fresh dill, fresh garlic with parsley, fresh chives and parsley, freshly ground black pepper or fresh rosemary. Use whatever you favor and invent your own combinations.

Flat Bread with Sesame Topping, Salmon and Dill Butter, Pecorino and Herb Butter, Mustard Pepperoni Butter

FLAT BREAD WITH SESAME TOPPING

> *6 tablespoons butter, softened*
>
> *3 tablespoons mixed dried herbs*
>
> *8 flat bread rounds, cut into large wedges*
>
> *¼ cup sesame seeds*

Preheat oven to 350°F.

Melt butter in a small saucepan and stir through herbs.

Brush butter mixture over flat breads. Place on a baking sheet and sprinkle with sesame seeds.

Bake for 15 minutes or until crisp.

SERVES 8

MUSTARD PEPPERONI BUTTER

> *4 ounces (1 stick) butter, softened*
>
> *3 ounces pepperoni, finely chopped (about ⅓ cup)*
>
> *1 tablespoon mustard*
>
> *1 tablespoon chopped chives*

Place butter in a small bowl and beat until light and smooth.

Stir through pepperoni, mustard and chives. Chill until ready to use. Serve with barbecued vegetables and meats.

SALMON AND DILL BUTTER

> *4 ounces (1 stick) butter, softened*
>
> *2 ounces smoked salmon, chopped (about ¼ cup)*
>
> *3 to 4 tablespoons chopped fresh dill*
>
> *1 tablespoon freshly ground pepper*

Place butter in a bowl and beat until light and smooth.

Mix in salmon, dill and pepper. Chill until ready to use. Serve with bread or on barbecued vegetables or meats.

PECORINO AND HERB BUTTER

> *4 ounces (1 stick) butter, softened*
>
> *¼ cup grated Pecorino cheese*
>
> *¼ cup chopped fresh mixed herbs*
>
> *1 tablespoon freshly ground pepper*

Place butter in a small bowl and beat until light and smooth.

Mix in cheese, herbs and pepper. Chill until ready to use. Serve with barbecued vegetables or meats.

CHILI BUTTER

> *4 ounces (1 stick) butter, softened*
>
> *1 to 2 teaspoons cayenne*
>
> *few drops hot pepper sauce*
>
> *1 tablespoon tomato paste*

Place butter in a small bowl and beat until light and smooth.

Stir through cayenne, hot pepper sauce and tomato paste. Chill until ready to use. Great served with hamburgers and meats.

FRUIT AND TEA DAMPER

½ cup chopped dried apricots

½ cup chopped raisins

¾ cup dates, pitted and chopped

finely grated rind of 1 orange

2 cups warm tea

4 tablespoons butter, softened

1 teaspoon allspice

3 tablespoons sugar

*1 quantity damper dough
(see below)*

Combine fruits in a small bowl, cover with tea and set aside for 30 minutes to soak. Drain very well then combine with butter, allspice and sugar.

Preheat oven to 400°F.

Pat damper dough out to form a circle approximately 12 inches in diameter. Place fruit in the center. Fold edges of circle towards center (the circle should now be a square) and pinch edges together to encase filling.

Carefully place fruit damper on a greased baking sheet and brush lightly with a little beaten egg. Bake for 25 minutes. Reduce heat to 350°F and bake 15 to 20 minutes more, or until well risen.

Cool slightly before serving, otherwise the filling will be too hot.

SERVES 8

DAMPER

4 cups self-rising flour

1 teaspoon salt

2 tablespoons butter

1 cup milk

½ cup water

Preheat oven to 400°F.

Sift flour and salt into a large bowl. Rub butter through flour with fingertips.

Damper, Fruit and Tea Damper

Make a well in the center and add milk and water. Mix until it forms a soft dough.

Turn out on a floured board and knead until smooth. Form dough into a large round.

Place on a greased and floured baking sheet and bake for 25 to 35 minutes or until top is browned and bread sounds hollow when tapped.

SERVES 8

HAM AND BLUE CHEESE BREAD

1 loaf of bread of your choice

FILLING

7 tablespoons butter, softened

2 ounces ham, finely sliced

2 ounces (4 tablespoons) creamy blue veined cheese

3 tablespoons chopped fresh parsley

1 tablespoon freshly ground pepper

Preheat oven to 400°F.

Cut bread into thick slices.

To Make Filling: Mix the butter, ham, cheese, parsley and pepper.

Spread slices with filling and reassemble the loaf. Wrap in foil and bake for 10 minutes.

Open top of foil and bake 10 minutes more or until loaf is crisp.

SERVES 6 TO 8

BARBECUE BREADS

Just about any bread goes with a barbecue. French bread sticks are hard to beat and so are whole wheat bread rolls, rye, black bread, braids, herb breads and sour dough. Few people have time to make bread these days and there is really no need as there are some excellent breads in the markets. You can transform the average bread loaf into something special with herbed and savory butters. For special occasions make damper or buttermilk bread — so easy and it makes a great impression. Add a handful of your favorite herbs to the mixture for something different.

CHEESE AND CHIVE BREAD

1 loaf of bread of your choice

FILLING

4 tablespoons butter, softened

One 3-ounce package cream cheese

4 ounces (1 cup) grated cheddar cheese

3 tablespoons chopped fresh parsley

¼ cup chopped fresh chives

1 teaspoon freshly ground pepper

Preheat oven to 400°F.

Cut bread into thick slices.

To Make Filling: Mix the butter, cheeses, parsley, chives and pepper.

Spread slices with filling and reassemble the loaf. Wrap in foil and bake for 10 minutes.

Open top of foil and bake for a further 10 minutes or until loaf is crisp and cheese has melted.

SERVES 6 TO 8

GARLIC AND HERB BREAD

1 loaf of Italian or French bread

FILLING

7 tablespoons butter, softened

3 cloves garlic, crushed

about 2 tablespoons chopped fresh mixed herbs

1 tablespoon Worcestershire sauce

1 tablespoon freshly ground pepper

4 ounces (1 cup) grated cheddar cheese

Preheat oven to 400°F.

Cut bread into slices but not all the way through.

To Make Filling: Mix the butter, garlic, herbs, Worcestershire and pepper.

Spread slices with filling and wrap loaf in foil. Bake for 10 minutes.

Open top of foil and sprinkle loaf with cheese. Return to oven for 10 minutes or until cheese melts.

SERVES 6 TO 8

BUTTERMILK BREAD

2 cups whole wheat flour

2¼ cups unbleached flour

1 teaspoon salt

2½ teaspoons bicarbonate of soda

1¼ cups buttermilk

Preheat oven to 450°F.

Sift flours, salt and bicarbonate of soda and stir in buttermilk a little at a time. Beat until dough is firm and leaves sides of bowl clean. Turn onto floured surface and knead until smooth.

Shape into flattish round loaf 8 inches in diameter. Place on a greased baking sheet and, using a sharp knife, cut a deep cross in the top. Bake for 25 to 30 minutes or until loaf sounds hollow when tapped.

SERVES 4

PATAFLA

1 baguette or long French stick

FILLING

6 tomatoes, peeled and chopped

6 scallions, finely chopped

2 green peppers, chopped

1 red pepper, chopped

7 ounces (1½ cups) black olives, pitted and chopped

1 tablespoon capers, chopped

4 gherkins, chopped

1 tablespoon freshly ground pepper

1 tablespoon grain mustard

Cut bread in half lengthwise. Scoop out most of the soft bread.

To Make Filling: Mix together the tomatoes, scallions, peppers, olives, capers, gherkins, pepper and mustard.

Spoon filling into hollowed bread. Press both halves together, wrap in foil and refrigerate for 1 hour. To serve, cut into slices.

SERVES 10

FRENCH ONION LOAF

1 loaf French or Italian bread

FILLING

8 ounces (1 cup) cream cheese

1 packet French onion soup mix

Preheat oven to 400°F.

Cut bread into thick slices.

To Make Filling: Combine the cream cheese and soup mix.

Spread slices with filling and reassemble loaf. Wrap in foil and bake for 10 minutes.

Open top of foil and bake for a further 10 minutes or until loaf is crisp.

SERVES 6 TO 8

CHEESE AND BACON LOAF

3 cups self-rising flour

1 teaspoon salt

4 tablespoons butter

1 cup milk

FILLING

2 slices cooked bacon, crumbled

4 ounces (1 cup) grated cheddar cheese

1 tablespoon grainy mustard

½ teaspoon paprika

1 egg, lightly beaten

Preheat oven to 400°F.

Sift flour and salt into a large bowl. Rub butter through flour with fingertips.

Make a well in the center and add milk. Mix to form a smooth dough. Turn onto a floured board and knead lightly. Roll out dough to form a 12 x 10-inch rectangle.

To Make Filling: Combine the bacon, cheese, mustard and paprika. Spread filling over dough, and beginning at the long edge, roll into a loaf.

Place loaf on a greased baking sheet, brush with egg and bake for 20 to 30 minutes.

SERVES 6

Clockwise from bottom left: French Onion Loaf, Patafla, Cheese and Bacon Loaf

Plate and bowl from Pill____ ____ass and napkins
from Orrefors Kosta Boda ____ ____des

In the Shade of the Garden

*O*n a hot summer's day, sit back and relax under the shade of a tree and treat yourself and your guests to these delicious dishes, that are so easy to make. Take lunch or a late afternoon break in the garden in gourmet style.

SMOKED CHICKEN FOCACCIA

4 squares focaccia, split in half

4 smoked chicken breasts, filleted

4 ounces sun dried peppers, sliced

2 peaches, sliced

8 curly lettuce leaves

¼ cup mayonnaise

Fill focaccia with chicken, peppers and peaches. Toast until warm. Top with lettuce and mayonnaise and serve.

SERVES 4

ASPARAGUS AND GORGONZOLA SLICE

2 bunches asparagus

¼ cup chopped chives

4 ounces (½ cup) Gorgonzola cheese, crumbled

1 cup self-rising flour

4 tablespoons butter, melted

5 eggs

1 cup milk

1 teaspoon freshly ground pepper

Preheat oven to 350°F.

Lightly steam asparagus until tender. Mix the chives, Gorgonzola, flour, butter, eggs, milk and pepper.

Place asparagus in a greased 8 inch square pan. Pour over egg mixture and bake for 30 to 40 minutes or until set and golden brown. Serve warm or cold.

SERVES 6

Picture previous pages: Ratatouille Tart, Warm Summer Pasta, Smoked Salmon Sandwiches (recipes page 55)

Below: Asparagus and Gorgonzola Slice

SMOKED SALMON SANDWICHES

8 large slices smoked salmon

½ bunch watercress, tips only

8 slices bread or 4 rolls

LIME MAYONNAISE

½ cup mayonnaise

1 tablespoon fresh lime juice

1 tablespoon finely sliced lime zest

1 teaspoon cracked pepper

Arrange smoked salmon and watercress on bread.

To Make Lime Mayonnaise: Mix mayonnaise, lime juice and zest and pepper.

Spoon mayonnaise over salmon and retreat to a quiet corner of the garden to eat.

SERVES 4

RATATOUILLE TART

PASTRY

8 tablespoons (1 stick) butter, cut in pieces

2 cups unbleached flour

1 egg

1 to 3 tablespoons water

RATATOUILLE

2 eggplants, diced

salt

2 red onions, chopped

1 tablespoon olive oil

2 cloves garlic, crushed

2 green peppers, chopped

4 zucchini, chopped

5 tomatoes, peeled, seeded and chopped

3 tablespoons chopped fresh basil

3 tablespoons chopped fresh oregano

freshly ground pepper

4 ounces (1 cup) grated aged cheddar

To Make Pastry: Place butter and flour in a food processor and process until mixture resembles fine crumbs. Add the egg and enough water to form a soft dough. Knead pastry lightly, cover with plastic wrap and refrigerate for 30 minutes.

Preheat oven to 350°F.

Roll pastry to fit a 12 inch quiche pan. Prick base and sides and bake for 15 minutes or until crisp and golden.

To Prepare Ratatouille: Place eggplant in a colander and sprinkle with salt. Allow to drain for 20 minutes. Rinse and dry.

Sauté onions in oil until golden brown. Add garlic, peppers, zucchini, tomatoes, eggplant, herbs, and pepper to taste. Simmer for 30 to 40 minutes. Cool slightly.

Pour into quiche shell. Sprinkle with cheese and return to oven for 12 minutes or until cheese melts. Serve warm or cold.

SERVES 6 TO 8

WARM SUMMER PASTA

5 tomatoes, peeled and chopped

8 sun dried tomatoes, sliced

2 ounces (½ cup) pitted black olives, chopped

¼ cup chopped basil

3 tablespoons balsamic vinegar

1 pound fettucine or tagliatelle pasta

1 tablespoon olive oil

2 cloves garlic, crushed

3 tablespoons chopped fresh sage

6 slices spicy salami, cut into strips (about ½ cup)

grated Parmesan cheese, to serve

Mix the tomatoes, olives, basil and vinegar and let stand for 30 minutes.

Cook pasta in boiling water until tender, drain and keep warm.

Heat oil in a large pan and sauté garlic, sage and salami until garlic is golden. Remove from heat and toss with pasta and tomato mixture. Serve warm with Parmesan cheese and bread.

SERVES 4 TO 6

MUSHROOM AND ROASTED PEPPER RISOTTO

¼ cup butter

2 cloves garlic, crushed

1 onion, finely chopped

8 ounces button mushrooms, halved

2 cups arborio rice

8 to 10 cups hot chicken or vegetable stock

1 red pepper, halved

1 green pepper, halved

3 tablespoons chopped chives

freshly ground pepper

In a large pan, sauté garlic and onion in butter until brown. Add mushrooms and cook for 1 minute.

Add rice to pan and cook until grains become milky. Stir in 2 cups of stock. Continue to add stock in lessening amounts, while stirring, until stock is absorbed.

Grill peppers until charred and soft. Peel away skins and chop. Stir through risotto with chives and freshly ground pepper, and serve.

SERVES 6

COCONUT ROUGH COOKIES

2 egg whites

1 cup shredded coconut

⅔ cup confectioner's sugar

1 teaspoon vanilla extract

3 ounces (½ cup) grated white chocolate

Preheat oven to 400°F.

Mix the egg whites, coconut, confectioner's sugar, vanilla and chocolate, until a stiff paste is formed.

Place spoonfuls of mixture on baking sheets and bake for 12 to 15 minutes or until light golden brown. Serve with scented tea.

MAKES 20

TANGELO SYRUP CAKE

½ pound (2 sticks) butter

3 tablespoons grated tangelo rind

1 cup sugar

3 eggs, separated

2 cups self-rising flour, sifted

½ cup buttermilk

½ cup yogurt

1 teaspoon vanilla extract

TANGELO SYRUP

4 tablespoons tangelo juice

¾ cup sugar

¼ cup water

Preheat oven to 375°F.

Beat together butter, grated rind and sugar until light and creamy. Add egg yolks and beat well. Mix in flour, buttermilk, yogurt and vanilla.

Beat egg whites until they stand in soft peaks and fold through mixture. Pour into a greased 8-inch round cake tin and bake for 1 hour or until a skewer inserted in the middle comes out clean.

To Make Tangelo Syrup: Place juice, sugar and water in a small pan and stir over low heat until sugar dissolves. Simmer syrup for 3 minutes.

Pour hot syrup over hot, turned-out cake. Serve warm with cream.

SERVES 8

BABY LEMON MERINGUE PIES

LEMON FILLING

8 tablespoons (1 stick) butter

1 cup sugar

2 eggs, lightly beaten

½ cup fresh lemon juice

12 small ready-made pastry shells

MERINGUE TOPPING

3 egg whites

¾ cup superfine sugar

To Make Lemon Filling: Put butter, sugar, eggs and lemon juice in the top of a double boiler. Stir over low heat until mixture is thick. Cool and pour into pastry shells.

To Make Meringue: Beat egg whites until soft peaks are formed. Gradually add sugar, beating well. Top pies with a generous spoonful of meringue. Brown quickly under a medium broiler or a salamander.

MAKES 12

Baby Lemon Meringue Pies, Tangelo Syrup Cake

Portable Picnics

A picnic is often a spur-of-the-moment meal, thrown together from staples found in the pantry, so the family can take advantage of an unexpectedly fine day. But with a small amount of forethought and planning, a picnic can become a treat, with any setting you choose. Spread out the blanket, or take the table and chairs, add some sparkling wine or fruit juice, and the picnic turns into an outdoor feast.

Basket and rug from Country Road, plates from Accoutrement, glass from Orrefors Kosta Boda

SESAME CHEESE PIE

1 pound ricotta cheese

1¼ cups sour cream

2 eggs, lightly beaten

4 ounces (1 cup) grated cheddar cheese

4 scallions, chopped

3 tablespoons chopped fresh mint

1 bunch chives, chopped

1 package prepared puff pastry

1 additional egg, lightly beaten

3 tablespoons sesame seeds

Preheat oven to 375°F.

Mix the ricotta, sour cream, eggs, cheese, onions, mint and chives.

Roll half of the puff pastry to form a rectangle 7 x 13 inches and place on a baking sheet. Cover with filling leaving a 1-inch border. Roll remaining half of pastry to fit over filling. Brush edges with extra egg and press edges together.

Make a few cuts in the top of the pastry to allow steam to escape. Brush with egg and sprinkle with sesame seeds. Bake for 25 to 35 minutes or until golden brown. Serve warm or cold, cut into wedges.

SERVES 6

STACKED PICNIC LOAF

1 loaf of Italian or Viennese bread

HAM FILLING

8 slices smoked delicatessen ham

¼ cup pickles

1 small cucumber, sliced

1 red pepper, sliced

CHEESE FILLING

8 slices Swiss cheese

2 tomatoes, sliced

1 head leaf lettuce, shredded

1 carrot, grated

Cut 8 slices in the loaf but not all the way through. Put a piece of ham between the first two slices. Spread with pickles, cucumber and pepper.

Fill the next two slices with cheese, tomato, lettuce and carrot. Repeat fillings until done.

SERVES 4 TO 6

POTATO AND BACON SALAD

3 slices cooked bacon, crumbled

2 ½ pounds new potatoes, cooked and cooled

¼ cup good quality salad dressing

1 cup mayonnaise

3 tablespoons chopped fresh chives

1 teaspoon freshly ground pepper

Peel potatoes and cut into small pieces.

Mix the salad dressing, mayonnaise, chives and pepper and pour over potatoes. Add bacon, toss, and chill until ready to serve.

SERVES 6

SPINACH TORTILLA

Tortillas are Spanish-style omelets and make great, easily transportable picnic food.

1 tablespoon olive oil

1 red onion, chopped

2 potatoes, peeled and chopped

8 spinach leaves, shredded

¾ cup light sour cream

6 eggs, lightly beaten

1 teaspoon freshly ground pepper

3 tablespoons chopped fresh parsley

Heat oil in a large, non-stick fry pan. Add onion and potatoes and sauté over low heat until soft. Add spinach leaves and cook until wilted.

Mix sour cream, eggs, pepper and parsley and pour into pan. Cook over low heat until almost set. Place under a hot broiler to brown the top.

Allow to cool in pan. Turn tortilla out of pan and serve cut into wedges with crusty bread.

SERVES 6

SAND-WEDGES

1 large round rye bread

FILLING

4 tablespoons ready-made pesto

12 slices spicy salami

4 tomatoes, sliced

12 thick slices Camembert

12 spinach leaves

1 yellow pepper, sliced

1 cucumber, thinly sliced

Cut top off bread. Scoop out soft bread filling, leaving a 1-inch shell. Spread inside of bread with pesto.

Layer half the salami, tomatoes, Camembert, spinach, pepper and cucumber. Repeat the layers. Replace the top and tie securely with string. Cut into wedges to serve.

SERVES 6

Previous pages: Stacked Picnic Loaf (page 60), Spinach Tortilla (page 60), Peach and Raspberry Tarts (page 67)

PORK AND VEAL TERRINE

1 onion, finely chopped

1 clove garlic, crushed

1 teaspoon butter

2 pounds ground pork and veal

½ pound (about ½ pint) chicken livers, finely chopped

2 eggs, lightly beaten

1 tablespoon chopped fresh sage

1 teaspoon fresh thyme

¼ cup brandy

1 teaspoon freshly ground pepper

8 slices bacon

Preheat oven to 350°F.

Sauté onion and garlic in butter until soft. Mix the ground meats, livers, eggs, sage, thyme, brandy and pepper.

Line a terrine dish with overlapping slices of bacon. Press mixture into terrine and fold overlapping bacon slices over mixture to seal. Cover with foil and place terrine in a deep baking dish. Add enough water to come halfway up the sides of the terrine.

Bake for 1½ hours or until juices are clear. Drain any excess liquid from terrine and refrigerate until cold. Serve sliced with crusty bread.

SERVES 8

Pork and Veal Terrine, Potato and Bacon Salad

SHRIMP AND CHEESE TARTS

PASTRY

- 1½ cups flour
- 7 tablespoons butter
- ½ cup grated cheddar cheese
- 3 tablespoons cold water

FILLING

- 6 ounces (about ½ cup) chopped cooked shrimp
- 4 ounces (1 cup) grated tasty cheese
- 2 scallions, chopped
- 4 eggs, lightly beaten
- ½ cup cream
- ½ cup milk
- 1 tablespoon grated lemon rind
- 1 teaspoon freshly ground pepper

Preheat oven to 375°F.

Place flour and butter in a food processor and process until mixture resembles fine bread crumbs. Add cheese and enough water to form a smooth dough.

Knead pastry lightly on a floured board. Roll dough thinly and cut into 24 2½-inch rounds. Press pastry into patty tins.

Put a small spoonful of shrimp in each shell. Mix the cheese, onions, eggs, cream, milk, rind and pepper and pour over the shrimp. Bake for 15 to 20 minutes or until puffed and golden. Serve warm or cold.

SERVES 6 TO 8

POCKET PASTRIES

- 1 package filo pastry
- ½ pound (2 sticks) butter, melted

SEAFOOD FILLING

- 2 ounces (¼ cup) cottage cheese
- 8 ounces fresh or canned crab meat
- 2 scallions, chopped
- 1 teaspoon freshly ground pepper

CHEESE AND SPINACH FILLING

- 6 spinach leaves, shredded and cooked
- 1 small onion, chopped
- 2 ounces feta cheese
- ½ teaspoon fresh lemon juice
- ½ teaspoon freshly ground pepper

CHILI MEAT FILLING

- ¼ pound cooked ground meat
- 1 tablespoon chili sauce
- 1 tablespoon tomato paste
- 1 small onion, chopped

CREAM CHEESE FILLING

- 4 ounces cream cheese, softened (about ½ cup)
- 2 scallions, chopped
- 1 tablespoon grainy mustard
- ½ teaspoon freshly ground pepper

Preheat oven to 400°F.

To Prepare Fillings: Mix the relevant ingredients in separate bowls.

Take 2 sheets of pastry and place one on top of the other. Cut pastry into 6 equal strips across the width. Brush each piece with a little butter.

Place a spoonful of the selected filling in a corner of the pastry. Fold over the other corner to form a triangle shape. Keep folding in a triangle shape to the edge of pastry. Brush pastry triangle with butter.

Repeat with remaining sheets of pastry and fillings.

Bake for 15 to 20 minutes or until golden.

MAKES ABOUT 30

FILO PASTRY

If you are using frozen filo pastry, make sure you thaw it first. Frozen pastry is brittle and breaks easily. Leave it unopened at room temperature for about 3 hours before using. If you are using chilled filo, leave it at room temperature for 1 to 2 hours.

While you are preparing the filling, cover the pastry with a dry cloth then a moist one to prevent the pastry from drying out. Don't let the pastry come into direct contact with the wet cloth as the sheets will stick together.

Brush pastry sheets with butter for a rich flavor, especially if you are making a dessert. But if you are watching your cholesterol intake, use olive oil. This is best used on savory pastries.

Shrimp and Cheese Tarts, Pocket Pastries

SAGE AND ONION ROLLS

1 tablespoon olive oil

1 onion, finely chopped

1 pound ground beef

¼ cup chopped fresh sage

3 tablespoons chopped fresh parsley

1 teaspoon freshly ground pepper

½ pound prepared piecrust pastry

1 egg, lightly beaten

Preheat oven to 375°F.

Sauté onion in olive oil until soft. Scrape into a bowl and mix with the ground beef, sage, parsley and pepper.

Cut prepared pastry in half. Roll each piece into a 14 x 5-inch rectangle. Place the filling down the center of each pastry piece.

Brush edges with beaten egg and bring pastry over filling and overlap slightly to form a roll. Cut each roll into 6 individual rolls and brush with egg.

Place rolls on a baking tray and bake for 15 minutes or until golden and cooked. Serve warm or cold.

SERVES 6

ITALIAN BEEF ROULADE

Two 1-pound pieces rump steak

FILLING

6 slices prosciutto

8 sun dried tomatoes, chopped

2 ounces (⅔ cup) pitted black olives, chopped

3 tablespoons chopped basil

6 artichoke hearts, finely chopped

2 cups fresh bread crumbs

1 tablespoon green peppercorns

Preheat oven to 400°F.

Trim fat from steaks. Pound until ½ inch thick. Overlap pieces of steak to form one large piece, and cover with prosciutto.

To Prepare Filling: Mix the tomatoes, olives, basil, artichokes, bread crumbs and peppercorns.

Place filling down the center and roll meat around to form a tight package. Tie with string and place on a baking tray. Bake for 1 hour or until cooked through. Allow to cool. Slice and serve.

SERVES 6 TO 8

SUN DRIED TOMATOES

Sun dried tomatoes can be purchased in the dried form or marinated in oil, often with garlic, herbs or spices. They have a very concentrated flavor and a dark red color. If you buy them dried, soak them in warm water for at least 30 minutes before using.

Italian Beef Roulade

CHOCOLATE NUT SLICE

- 8 tablespoons (1 stick) butter
- ½ cup brown sugar
- 1 tablespoon golden syrup or light corn syrup
- 3 tablespoons cocoa
- 1 egg, beaten
- ½ teaspoon vanilla
- 1 cup crushed sugar cookies (about 7 ounces)
- ½ cup chopped nuts (walnuts, almonds or pecans)
- 3 tablespoons desiccated coconut

ICING

- 3 ounces semi-sweet chocolate
- ¼ cup water
- 1 teaspoon oil
- 2 cups confectioner's sugar, sifted
- ¼ cup finely chopped nuts (walnuts, almonds or pecans)

Combine butter, sugar, golden syrup and cocoa in saucepan. Stir over low heat to dissolve sugar, then heat until bubbling.

Remove from heat and add beaten egg and vanilla, stirring until thick. Add crushed biscuits, nuts and coconut and mix well. Press mixture into greased small baking tin, about 7 x 11-inches. Chill until firm.

To Make Icing: Combine chocolate, water and oil in the top of a double boiler, and stir over hot water until chocolate melts. Add confectioner's sugar and mix well.

Spread chocolate icing over mixture in pan and sprinkle with nuts. Allow icing to set before cutting into squares or fingers to serve.

MAKES ABOUT 20

FRUIT STRUDEL JAFFLES

Try different types of canned fruit instead of apple.

- 1 pound canned pie apples
- ¾ cup golden raisins
- ¼ cup chopped raisins
- 1 tablespoon grated lemon rind
- ½ cup chopped walnuts
- 1 tablespoon apple pie spice
- 3 tablespoons sugar
- 2 packages prepared shortcrust pastry (about 2 pounds)
- 3 tablespoons butter, melted

Combine the apples, raisins, lemon rind, walnuts, spice and sugar.

Cut pastry sheets according to size of electric sandwich maker. Grease with a little butter and place a square of pastry in sandwich maker. Top with spoonfuls of filling and a square of pastry.

Brush the top square of pastry with a little butter and close lid. Cook for 4 to 5 minutes or until golden. Repeat with remaining pastry and filling.

SERVES 6

SHORTCRUST PASTRY

Shortcrust pastry is usually used for pies, tarts and turnovers.
Although easy to make, it is a lot more convenient to buy from the supermarket frozen and ready rolled.

PEACH AND RASPBERRY TARTS

- 3 sheets prepared puff pastry
- 4 tablespoons butter
- 4 tablespoons chopped roasted hazelnuts
- ¼ cup sugar
- 1 teaspoon ground cinnamon
- 4 to 6 peaches, peeled and sliced
- ½ pint raspberries
- extra sugar

Preheat oven to 425°F.

Cut each pastry sheet into 4 squares. With pastry cutter or sharp knife cut the middle out of 6 pastry squares. Reserve middles for another recipe.

Dampen the edges of the full squares, and lay a cut square over each.

Beat together butter, hazelnuts, sugar and cinnamon. Spread inside each pastry case.

Top with slices of peach and raspberries. Sprinkle with extra sugar and place on baking tray. Bake for 12 to 15 minutes or until golden and crisp.

Cool, store and transport to your picnic in an airtight container.

MAKES 6

Fruit Strudel Jaffles

Packing a Picnic

For a purely portable picnic, the most
versatile article you could buy is a picnic
basket. Those with a lid are best —
saving those bottles from rolling out as
you walk down to the park!

These days picnic sets can be bought
from housewares stores and department
stores with the latest in picnic accessories.
Non-breakable plates and cups come in
a wide range of colors with cutlery
to match.

A tablecloth is always a classy touch
at a picnic — transport the dining
room outside!

Something on the Side

Gone are the days of the limp lettuce leaf, sliced cucumber and tomato smothered with salad dressing. The average supermarket, and of course the well-stocked vegetable market, provide a stunning array of vegetables and fruit which with imagination and experience can enhance any meal. Salads are limited only by your personal preferences, and to know that you are eating healthily is an added bonus.

Bowls from Country Road, fabric from Les Olivades

Salads

Salad making provides year-round opportunities for invention. Serve two or three with different dressings, or arrange prepared salad vegetables on large platters with separate bowls of mayonnaise or dressings so your guests can help themselves. Salads don't have to be served with the main meal. They can stand alone.

The amount of dressing doesn't need to double when you double the recipe. You only need a little dressing tossed through a salad to give it taste. Too much and everything gets soggy.

SALAD NIÇOISE

A slight twist on the traditional version.

⅓ pound baby green beans, blanched

8 artichoke hearts, halved

½ cup pitted black olives

2 tomatoes, cut into wedges

8 sun dried tomatoes, halved

3 hard-boiled eggs, quartered

3 tablespoons chopped fresh basil

DRESSING

¼ cup olive oil

3 tablespoons balsamic vinegar

1 tablespoon grainy mustard

3 tablespoons chopped fresh parsley

Arrange beans, artichokes, olives, tomatoes, eggs and basil on a serving platter.

To Prepare Dressing: Combine oil, vinegar, mustard and parsley. Pour over salad and toss lightly to combine. Chill until required.

SERVES 6

MIXED GREENS WITH BLUE CHEESE DRESSING

Simple but delicious. For ideas on greens to use, see our salad greens identification picture on page 86. Use a variety of lettuces, endive and cress.

mixed salad greens

BLUE CHEESE DRESSING

4 ounces soft blue cheese, like Gorgonzola

¼ cup olive oil

¼ cup yogurt

1 tablespoon white wine vinegar

1 teaspoon freshly ground pepper

Place greens in a serving bowl.

To Make Dressing: Put cheese, oil, yogurt, vinegar and pepper in a blender and blend until smooth. Chill.

When ready to serve, pour dressing over salad greens.

SERVES 6

KING OF CAESAR SALAD

2 heads romaine lettuce

6 slices bacon, chopped

1½ cups croutons

1 pint cherry tomatoes, halved

1 avocado, sliced

DRESSING

½ cup olive oil

4 anchovies

2 cloves garlic, crushed

1 egg

1 tablespoon freshly ground pepper

3 tablespoons fresh lemon juice

1 tablespoon grainy mustard

¼ cup raspberry or red wine vinegar

½ cup freshly shaved Parmesan cheese

Break lettuce into large pieces and arrange on a serving platter. Sauté bacon until crisp and drain on absorbent paper. Add bacon to salad with croutons, tomatoes and avocado.

To Make Dressing: Put oil, anchovies, garlic, egg and pepper in a blender and blend until smooth. Gradually add lemon juice, mustard and vinegar. Pour dressing over salad, toss and top with Parmesan cheese.

SERVES 6 TO 8

Picture previous pages: Left to right: King of Caesar Salad, Salad Niçoise (recipes page 72)

CITRUS MANGO SALAD

1 head iceberg lettuce

3 oranges, peeled and sectioned

3 celery stalks, sliced

2 mangoes, peeled and sliced

1 cucumber, sliced

6 scallions, thinly sliced

DRESSING

¼ cup mayonnaise

¼ cup sour cream

3 tablespoons chopped fresh parsley

1 teaspoon Dijon mustard

1 tablespoon fresh orange juice

1 tablespoon fresh lemon juice

Place lettuce, oranges, celery, mangoes, cucumber and scallions on a serving platter.

Citrus Mango Salad

To Make Dressing: Combine the mayonnaise, sour cream, parsley, mustard and juices.

Pour dressing over salad and serve chilled.

SERVES 6 TO 8

ROASTED VEGETABLE SALAD

1 large eggplant, cut in
  lengthwise slices

salt

2 red peppers, cut in half

olive oil

1 red onion, sliced

1 head leaf lettuce

DRESSING

3 ounces soft blue-veined cheese

1 tablespoon sour cream

¼ cup cream

3 tablespoons chopped fresh basil

Sprinkle eggplant with salt and let stand 30 minutes. Rinse slices and pat dry.

Place pepper halves, skin side up, and eggplant under a hot broiler. Brush well with oil. Grill peppers until skin is charred and blistered. Remove skin and slice. Grill eggplant slices until golden on both sides.

Arrange eggplant, peppers and onion over lettuce.

To Make Dressing: Combine cheese, sour cream, cream and basil. Pour over salad and chill until ready to serve.

SERVES 4

WARM SPINACH, ARTICHOKE AND PASTA SALAD

1 tablespoon olive oil

½ pound button mushrooms, sliced

4 scallions, sliced diagonally

1 bunch spinach, washed and
  torn into pieces

One 5½-ounce jar marinated
  artichoke hearts

2 cups dried shell pasta, cooked

¼ cup sun dried tomatoes

¼ cup grated Parmesan cheese

freshly ground pepper

Sauté mushrooms in oil for 2 to 3 minutes. Stir in onions and spinach. Cook until spinach just wilted.

Add undrained artichoke hearts and pasta and cook until heated through. Remove from heat and combine with tomatoes and Parmesan. Season to taste with plenty of pepper and serve.

SERVES 6

PROSCIUTTO AND SUGAR PEA SALAD

¼ cup oil

12 slices prosciutto, cut into
  slivers

1 tablespoon butter

½ pound sugar snap peas

1 head soft lettuce (Bibb or
  Boston), loosely torn

8 radicchio leaves

chives, snipped

Sauté prosciutto in oil until crisp. Drain on absorbent paper, and wipe pan.

In the same pan, heat butter until foaming, add peas and toss until bright green in color. Mix peas with lettuce, radicchio and prosciutto in a serving bowl and garnish with snipped chives.

SERVES 4

TROPICAL FRUITS WITH ZESTY LEMON DRESSING

3 mangoes

2 avocados

4 to 6 lettuce leaves

2 bananas, peeled and sliced
  lengthwise

1½ cups chopped macadamia nuts

ZESTY LEMON DRESSING

1 teaspoon chopped lemon zest

1 tablespoon fresh lemon juice

3 tablespoons olive oil

3 tablespoons safflower oil

cayenne pepper

salt

Peel mangoes and slice each lengthwise into 4 pieces. Peel avocados and cut into 5 or 6 slices.

Place lettuce leaves on serving plates and arrange the mango, banana and avocado slices decoratively on top.

To Make Zesty Lemon Dressing: Blend zest, juice, and oils, and add salt and cayenne to taste. Let stand 5 to 10 minutes to develop flavors before using.

Sprinkle fruit mixture with dressing and macadamia nuts.

SERVES 4 TO 6

Roasted Vegetable Salad, Warm Spinach, Artichoke and Pasta Salad, Prosciutto and Sugar Pea Salad

Marinated Beef Salad

MARINATED BEEF SALAD

¾ *pound sliced smoked beef*

¼ *cup fruity olive oil*

½ *cup red wine vinegar*

¼ *cup honey*

1 *tablespoon fresh chopped
  mixed herbs*

1 *cucumber, peeled and sliced*

½ *cup pitted black olives*

½ *bunch curly endive*

Place beef, oil, vinegar, honey and herbs in a small bowl. Cover and refrigerate for 1 hour.

Arrange beef, cucumber and olives on a bed of endive. Pour marinade over salad. Chill until required.

SERVES 6

WATERCRESS SALAD

1 bunch watercress

¼ pound mustard cress

½ bunch fresh spearmint, chopped

½ bunch chives, snipped

1 red onion, sliced

1 avocado, peeled and sliced

DRESSING

1 tablespoon mayonnaise

3 tablespoons herb vinegar

1 teaspoon green peppercorns

3 tablespoons chopped parsley

¼ cup olive oil

Wash watercress thoroughly, and remove young tips. Discard stalks. Arrange watercress tips, mustard cress, spearmint, chives, onion and avocado in a large serving bowl.

To Make Dressing: Whisk together the mayonnaise, vinegar, peppercorns, parsley and oil. Pour over salad just before serving.

SERVES 4

SPRING SALAD WITH CORIANDER DRESSING

1 small leaf lettuce

1 Belgian endive

1 bunch arugula

1 small bunch watercress

2 small radicchio, separated into leaves

8 small nasturtium leaves

¼ cup chervil sprigs (if available)

¼ cup Italian parsley sprigs

1 green pepper, sliced

1 pint cherry tomatoes

CORIANDER DRESSING

1 tablespoon Dijon mustard

¼ cup fresh lemon juice

6 tablespoons olive oil

¼ cup chopped fresh coriander

Wash and dry all the salad leaves. Arrange them in a salad bowl with the pepper and tomatoes.

To Make Dressing: Put mustard and lemon juice in a small bowl. Whisk in oil until mixture thickens. Stir through coriander and serve over salad.

SERVES 6

ROASTED VEGETABLES WITH STILTON DRESSING

4 potatoes, peeled and cubed

1 sweet potato, peeled and cubed

1 pound pumpkin, peeled and cubed

2 turnips, peeled and cubed

olive oil

3 sprigs rosemary

DRESSING

5 ounces Stilton cheese

½ cup yogurt

1 tablespoon fresh lemon juice

1 teaspoon freshly ground pepper

½ teaspoon ground cumin

Preheat oven to 400°F.

Place vegetables in a baking dish with oil and rosemary. Bake for 35 to 45 minutes or until cooked.

To Make Dressing: Combine Stilton, yogurt, juice, pepper and cumin in a blender and blend until smooth. Pour over hot or warm vegetables.

SERVES 4 TO 6

CRISP SALADS

To keep salads cool and crisp on a hot day when eating outside, place salad bowl in a larger bowl with some ice in the bottom.

RED CABBAGE SLAW WITH TAHINI ORANGE DRESSING

3 cups shredded red cabbage

1 cup shredded green cabbage

½ cup whole toasted blanched almonds

BASE DRESSING

3 tablespoons cream

1 tablespoon tarragon vinegar

1 teaspoon prepared mustard

¼ teaspoon salt

TAHINI ORANGE DRESSING

3 tablespoons tahini

3 tablespoons water

juice and finely grated rind 1 orange

Combine red and green cabbage, wash, drain and chill in refrigerator.

To Make Base Dressing: Combine ingredients in a jar and shake well.

Toss cabbage with dressing and half the almonds. Pile into salad bowl and top with the remaining almonds.

To Make Tahini Orange Dressing: Combine ingredients and pour over salad just before serving.

SERVES 6

NEW ITALIAN SALAD

1 curly endive

small bunch arugula

1 cup sun dried peppers, sliced

2 zucchini, cut into thin strips

½ pound bocconcini

¼ cup chopped purple basil

¼ cup olive oil

¼ cup balsamic vinegar

1 teaspoon freshly ground pepper

Arrange endive, arugula, peppers, zucchini, boconcini and basil on a serving plate.

Sprinkle with oil, vinegar and pepper. Cover, refrigerate and allow to stand for 1 hour before serving.

SERVES 6

ROASTED TOMATOES WITH PISTACHIO MINT PESTO

12 plum or egg tomatoes

olive oil

sea salt

freshly ground pepper

PISTACHIO MINT PESTO

½ cup (2 ounces shelled) pistachio nuts

½ cup mint leaves

2 cloves garlic, crushed

½ cup grated Parmesan cheese

¼ cup olive oil

Preheat oven to 350°F.

Halve tomatoes lengthwise and place skin side down on a baking dish. Sprinkle with oil, salt and pepper. Bake for 30 minutes or until soft.

To Prepare Pesto: Place pistachios, mint, garlic, Parmesan and oil in a blender and blend until very finely chopped. Serve with tomatoes.

SERVES 4 TO 6

AVOCADO AND LETTUCE SALAD WITH MUSTARD SEED DRESSING

2 avocados, peeled and sliced

juice ½ lemon

1 head lettuce

1 small cucumber, peeled and sliced

6 scallions, finely chopped

alfalfa sprouts

MUSTARD SEED DRESSING

3 tablespoons yogurt

1 tablespoon vegetable oil

1 tablespoon mustard seeds

1 teaspoon grated ginger

Sprinkle lemon juice over avocado. Wash and dry lettuce. Refrigerate 30 minutes until crisp then tear into bite-sized pieces. Place in salad bowl. Top with avocado slices. Add cucumber and garnish with scallions and alfalfa sprouts.

To Make Dressing: Combine all ingredients and mix until smooth. Just before serving, pour over salad and toss.

SERVES 8 TO 10

New Italian Salad, Roasted Tomatoes with Pistachio Mint Pesto

WARM SHREDDED CHICKEN SALAD

*4 skinless and boneless chicken
breasts*

1 tablespoon peanut oil

*3 tablespoons chopped fresh
coriander*

*2 tablespoons fresh lime or lemon
juice*

½ small cabbage, finely sliced

1 teaspoon sesame oil

3 tablespoons sesame seeds

8 radicchio leaves

Cut chicken into thin strips. Place
in a bowl with oil, coriander and
lime juice. Cover and stand for
20 minutes. Sauté in a hot pan for
4 minutes or until tender. Keep
warm.

Sauté cabbage in sesame oil with the
sesame seeds until wilted and tender.

Arrange radicchio on a serving
platter. Top with sesame cabbage
and chicken. Serve warm.

SERVES 4 TO 6

CARAMELIZED SWEET POTATOES

*3 sweet potatoes, peeled and cut
into large pieces*

6 small onions, halved

6 cloves garlic

4 tablespoons butter, melted

½ cup brown sugar, packed

¼ cup water

Preheat oven to 350°F.

Place potato pieces in a baking dish
with onions and garlic. Sprinkle
vegetables with butter, brown sugar
and water. Bake for 30 minutes or
until potatoes are soft and golden.

SERVES 6

THAI VEGETABLE SALAD

2 carrots, julienned

*1 bunch asparagus, halved and
lightly steamed*

4 scallions, sliced

8 large spinach leaves, chopped

1 red pepper, sliced

DRESSING

3 tablespoons chili oil

1 tablespoon sesame oil

¼ cup rice vinegar

¼ cup light soy sauce

Arrange carrots, asparagus, scallions,
spinach leaves and red pepper on a
serving platter.

To Make Dressing: Whisk together
the oils, vinegar and soy sauce. Pour
over salad and serve chilled.

SERVES 4

LENTIL SALAD WITH YOGURT DRESSING

1½ cups red lentils

2 cups chopped macadamia nuts

⅔ cup currants

4 scallions, sliced

*¼ pound mesclun or mixed
lettuce leaves*

YOGURT DRESSING

1 cup yogurt

3 tablespoons chopped fresh mint

1 clove garlic, crushed

3 tablespoons fresh lemon juice

3 tablespoons olive oil

Wash lentils until water runs clear.
Simmer in a large pot of water for
15 minutes or until just soft, drain
and cool.

Place lentils, nuts, currants, onions
and lettuce in a bowl and mix to
combine.

To Make Dressing: Whisk together
the yogurt, mint, garlic, lemon juice
and oil. Pour over salad and serve
chilled.

SERVES 4 TO 6

FENNEL AND ORANGE SALAD WITH TOMATO DRESSING

3 fennel bulbs

3 oranges

*3 tablespoons chopped fresh
parsley*

TOMATO DRESSING

1 cup tomato juice

juice 1 lime or ½ lemon

2 scallions, finely chopped

2 cloves garlic, chopped

Worcestershire sauce, to taste

hot pepper sauce, to taste

*freshly ground black pepper, to
taste*

Trim fennel bulbs and slice thinly.
Wash well and discard any discolored
slices. Cut both ends from oranges
then cut off all rind and pith. With a
small sharp knife, cut between
membranes of oranges and free
segments. Remove any seeds.

To Make Tomato Dressing: Combine
all ingredients and mix thoroughly.

Combine oranges, fennel and
Tomato Dressing. Cover and
refrigerate. Serve sprinkled with
parsley.

SERVES 10 TO 12

BARBECUED CHILI CORN

6 corn cobs with husks

4 tablespoons butter, melted

1 teaspoon chili powder

1 teaspoon ground cumin

1 teaspoon ground coriander

1 teaspoon freshly ground pepper

Remove most of the husks from the corn. Use the remaining husks to wrap around the base of the corn as a handle.

Brush corn with combined butter, chili, cumin, coriander and pepper. Barbecue until tender.

SERVES 6

Barbecued Chili Corn

From left to right: Raspberry Vinaigrette, Chili Vinaigrette, Herb Vinaigrette, Herb Mayonnaise, Tomato and Basil Mayonnaise

Dash or Splash

*W*hy buy a dressing when it's so easy to make your own and you can create the exact flavor you want? Once you've made a basic vinaigrette then you can make all kinds of combinations using herbs and spices of your choice.

Transform ordinary mayonnaise into a delicious dip or dressing, to serve with munchies, salads and on sandwiches.

BASIC VINAIGRETTE

¼ cup white wine vinegar

½ cup olive oil

1 teaspoon dry mustard

freshly ground black pepper

Put vinegar, oil, mustard and pepper in a jar and shake well to combine. Store in refrigerator until needed.

MAKES ½ CUP

CHILI VINAIGRETTE

¼ cup white wine vinegar

½ cup olive oil

1 teaspoon dry mustard

freshly ground black pepper

1 red chile pepper, seeded and finely chopped

1 tablespoon sweet chili sauce

Put vinegar, oil, mustard and pepper in a jar and shake well. Stir in chile and sweet chili sauce. Store in refrigerator until needed.

MAKES ½ CUP

HERB VINAIGRETTE

¼ cup white wine vinegar

½ cup olive oil

1 teaspoon powdered mustard

freshly ground black pepper to taste

1 tablespoon chopped fresh chives

1 tablespoon chopped fresh basil

1 tablespoon chopped fresh parsley

Put vinegar, oil, mustard and pepper in a jar and shake well. Stir through herbs. Store in refrigerator until needed.

MAKES ½ CUP

RASPBERRY VINAIGRETTE

¼ cup raspberry vinegar

½ cup olive oil

1 teaspoon powdered mustard

freshly ground black pepper to taste

Put vinegar, oil, mustard and pepper in a jar and shake well. Store in refrigerator until needed.

MAKES ½ CUP

VINEGAR

There are many kinds of vinegar available, including white wine, red wine, rice, apple cider and malt vinegar. Vinegar is an essential ingredient in salads, bringing out the flavor of the vegetables.

You can make your own herb-infused vinegar: Combine 1 quart of wine vinegar with ½ cup bruised fresh herbs of your choice in a glass or earthenware bowl. Cover and leave to infuse for 2 weeks. Strain through a double piece of cheesecloth into clean sterilized bottles. Add a sprig of the fresh herb to each bottle. Cork and label.

HERB MAYONNAISE

1 cup mayonnaise

3 tablespoons chopped fresh parsley

3 tablespoons chopped fresh chives

3 tablespoons chopped fresh basil

1 tablespoon freshly ground pepper

Combine the mayonnaise, parsley, chives, basil and pepper. Store in refrigerator.

Serve over salads, vegetables or barbecued meats.

MAKES 1 CUP

Making your own mayonnaise is too impractical for today's lifestyle, and good prepared mayonnaise is readily available almost everywhere. Use a good quality mayonnaise as a base for something more inspiring.

PESTO MAYONNAISE

1 cup mayonnaise

½ cup prepared pesto

1 teaspoon freshly ground pepper

Combine the mayonnaise, pesto and pepper. Store in the refrigerator.

Serve over salads, vegetables or barbecued meats.

MAKES 1 ½ CUPS

TOMATO AND BASIL MAYONNAISE

1 cup mayonnaise

3 tablespoons tomato paste

¼ cup chopped fresh basil

1 tablespoon freshly ground pepper

Combine the mayonnaise, tomato, basil and pepper. Store in the refrigerator.

Serve with salads, vegetables or barbecued meats.

MAKES 1 CUP

SWEET CURRY MAYONNAISE

1 cup mayonnaise

1 tablespoon ground cumin

1 teaspoon cayenne

3 tablespoons chopped fresh coriander

1 tablespoon curry powder

1 tablespoon brown sugar

Combine the mayonnaise, cumin, cayenne, coriander, curry powder and brown sugar. Store in the refrigerator.

Serve over salads, vegetables or barbecued meats.

MAKES 1 CUP

HERBED YOGURT DRESSING

1 cup low-fat yogurt

3 tablespoons chopped fresh parsley

1 tablespoon snipped fresh chives

1 tablespoon prepared mustard

salt and freshly ground black pepper

Combine yogurt, herbs and seasoning in a bowl. Chill before using. Use as needed.

MAKES 1 CUP

Almond, hazelnut and walnut oil have a good nutty flavor that complements many salads. Polyunsaturated oils such as corn oil, peanut oil, safflower oil and sunflower oil are light with little flavor and may be used in combination with one of the more full-bodied oils to lighten a particular dressing. Used alone they tend to lack flavor. Grapeseed oil is light and has a good nutty flavor. Olive oil is the most widely used and has a full flavor and smoothness that is very versatile. Extra virgin oil is the best. Sesame oil has a strong sesame flavor. Use sparingly as it can overpower the salad.

Make your own chili oil: Warm 2 cups of olive oil and pour into a clean bottle with 2 to 3 teaspoons chopped red chiles, or 1 or 2 dried red chiles. Cap and store in a cool, dark place for 2 weeks.

Make your own herb-infused oil: Warm 2 cups olive oil and pour into a clean jar with ¼ cup fresh herbs. Cover and leave for 2 weeks. Strain the oil through a fine cheesecloth into a bottle and store in a cool, dark place until required.

Salad Greens

1 Curly endive 2 Red leaf lettuce
3 Arugula 4 Radicchio 5 Leaf lettuce
6 Romaine lettuce 7 Red oak leaf lettuce
8 Watercress 9 Red butterhead lettuce

Salad Vegetables

Name	Description
Alfalfa sprouts	Sold in pints or loose and eaten at the seedling stage when full of vitamins and minerals.
Artichoke hearts	Sold in oil in jars, or canned in brine.
Artichokes	Artichokes make a good container for an individual salad. They resemble an unopened flower bud with tightly wrapped leaves.
Asparagus	Young shoot of a green plant. A popular addition to salads.
Avocado	This pear-shaped fruit has a delicate yet very distinctive flavor. Skin color varies from green to black depending on variety.
Baby squash	Eaten when very young and tender. Green or yellow in color. Similar in flavor to a baby zucchini.
Beans	Green, crisp pods with flavorsome seeds.
Bean sprouts	These are sprouted mung beans used when the sprout is about 1 inch long. Should be crisp and sweet-smelling when purchased.
Broccoli	Tight green florets on individual stems and a central stalk.
Chinese cabbage	Elongated cabbage with green-edged leaves. Heart nearly white.
Red cabbage	Round cabbage, deep red leaves.
Round head cabbage	Smooth pale green leaves.
Savoy cabbage	Has dark green wrinkled leaves with a firmly packed head.
White cabbage	Round, tight head.
Carrots	Use young, crisp carrots for salads.
Cauliflower	Tight head of white flower buds.

Storage	Preparation
Keep refrigerated as they continue to grow.	Simply pull required amount from pint.
Refrigerate after opening.	Delightful sliced into a salad.
Refrigerate in a plastic bag	Pull off any coarse outer leaves. Cut off top third of the artichoke and cook in boiling salted water (made slightly acidic with a dash of vinegar or squeeze of lemon juice) for 20–40 minutes, depending on their size. Remove hairy choke and serve filled with a vinaigrette dressing or fill with a salad of your choice.
Refrigerate in a plastic bag for 2 to 3 days.	Blanch in boiling, salted water and refresh before using or simply steam lightly. May be used whole if young, or cut into spears.
Store at room temperature until ripe then refrigerate for up to 3 days.	Eat at room temperature for full flavor. Slice just before using — otherwise rub the cut surfaces with lemon juice or vinaigrette.
Refrigerate for a few days.	Steam or stir fry before using in salads.
Refrigerate in a plastic bag for up to 5 days.	Crisp, young green runner beans need only trimming before use. May be sliced or left whole.
Refrigerate for up to 7 days.	Pinch off the dry, stringy end of the root before using.
Refrigerate in crisper for up to 5 days.	For salads, break into florets and blanch in boiling salted water. Drain and refresh under cold running water and dry well.
Refrigerate in a plastic bag for up to 7 days.	Crinkly leaves may be shredded and used raw.
Refrigerate in a plastic bag for up to 7 days.	Usually cooked with vinegar. May be finely shredded for coleslaw, adding a beautiful, purple-red color to the slaw.
Refrigerate in a plastic bag for up to 7 days.	Shred and use in coleslaw or steam and use in other salads.
Refrigerate in a plastic bag for up to 7 days.	Good shredded in coleslaw.
Refrigerate in a plastic bag for up to 7 days.	Usually used shredded for coleslaw or sauerkraut.
Refrigerate in a plastic bag with paper towel for up to 7 days.	Peel if necessary. Grate, julienne or leave whole if very small.
Remove tough leaves and refrigerate in crisper for up to 5 days.	For salads, break into florets and blanch in boiling salted water. Drain and refresh under cold, running water and dry well.

Salad Vegetables (continued)

Name	Description
Celery	Sold in whole or half heads. Leaf and stalk both edible.
Cucumbers	
White	Small, creamy white and oval-shaped.
Green	Smooth-skinned and dark green.
Kirby	Small, smooth-skinned green cucumber.
Gourmet	A long, thin, dark green variety of cucumber, crisp with a good flavor and few seeds.
Garlic	Choose firm, young white or purple bulbs when purchasing.
Kohlrabi	A cabbage—turnip type of vegetable, either purple or green in color. The thickened stem is eaten and has a delicate turnip flavor.
Long beans	Long, round-bodied thin bean. Similar in taste and texture to green bean. Sold in bunches.
Mushrooms	Use firm, white button mushrooms or caps in a salad.
Onions	
Scallion	These have a white bulb with long green tops. Sold in bunches. Mild onion flavor.
Spring onion	Similar to scallions but with a more pronounced bulb and onion flavor.
French shallot	Small brownish bulb with a soft onion flavor.
Italian red onion	Mild, sweet juicy onion with a red color which makes an attractive addition to salads.
White onion	Round, firm and white-fleshed with a dry white papery skin.
Pepper	May be green, red, yellow, even purple or chocolate. The sweet peppery flavor is very distinctive.
Radish	Firm, crisp, red bulbs, sold in bunches. Tops should be fresh-looking.
Tomatoes	Always use tomatoes at room temperature. Look for a good red color and firm flesh when using in salads. Whole cherry tomatoes or tom thumbs are a welcome addition to any salad. Also available are the small, yellow pear-shaped tomatoes, which have a good flavor.

Storage	Preparation
Refrigerate in a plastic bag for up to 7 days.	May be sliced or cut into sticks. For celery curls, cut 2-inch vertical slices halfway down each piece a few times. Repeat at other end and plunge into iced water. Leave until curled and crisp.
Wash and dry, store in crisper in refrigerator for up to 7 days.	Peel before using.
Wash and dry, store in crisper in refrigerator for up to 7 days.	Peel, leaving a little of the green skin (this is said to help with digestion). The surface may be scored with a fork. May be sliced into rounds or halved and seeded then sliced. Some people still like to lightly salt the slices to remove indigestible juices. Allow to stand for 30 minutes, drain and rinse well with cold water.
Wash and dry, store in crisper in refrigerator for up to 7 days.	Chop and use in salads. Drier than other cucumbers and good for pickles.
Wash and dry, store in crisper in refrigerator for up to 7 days.	Chop and use in salads.
Keep in a dry, airy place or peel cloves and keep in a jar of oil in the refrigerator.	Remove papery skin by crushing clove with back of a knife. Continue crushing and add a pinch salt. The salt acts as an abrasive to pulp the flesh while also absorbing pungent juices. Use a garlic press to crush if you prefer.
Refrigerate in a crisper for up to 7 days.	May be boiled or eaten raw. Add to salads grated or sliced. Delicious offset by horseradish.
Loosely wrap and refrigerate for up to 7 days.	Slice and blanch before using in a salad.
Refrigerate unwashed in a brown paper bag for up to 7 days.	Brush off any compost (don't rinse) and trim stalk end. Serve whole or sliced.
Refrigerate in a crisper.	Use white bulb with a little of the green stem finely chopped.
Refrigerate in a crisper.	Trim away roots and peel dry outer leaves before using.
Refrigerate in a crisper.	Used mainly in sautés.
Refrigerate in a crisper.	Peel outer leaves, chop or slice and add to salad.
Store in a cool, dry, dark place.	Peel before use. Strong, hot, pungent flavor. Use sparingly.
Refrigerate in crisper for up to 10 days.	Use raw or char skin and use cooked. Remove seeds and membranes and woody stem. Slice or chop.
Remove leaves, refrigerate in a plastic bag for up to 7 days.	Slice or serve whole with a few small green sprigs still attached. Remove stringy root.
Store at room temperature out of direct sunlight until ripe, then refrigerate for up to 5 days only.	Wash and dry. Slice or quarter for use in salads. Use cherry tomatoes whole.

Salad Greens

Name	Description	Flavour
Arugula	Small, dark green leaves with a pronounced. peppery flavor. Best eaten when young, as older arugula can be tough and bitter.	Acidic
Belgian endive or whitloof	Tightly clustered, smooth white leaves with yellow tips.	Slightly bitter
Curly endive	Sold in large bunches. The long leaves graduate from pale, greeny yellow to dark green. Use only the paler heart and stalks.	Bitter
Escarole	Long frilly leaves. Use only the center young leaves.	Slightly bitter
Butterhead lettuce	Soft, round lettuce with many varieties. Most common are Boston, Bibb and Buttercrunch.	Mild
Romaine or Cos lettuce	Elongated head of dark green oval leaves and a crisp pale green heart.	Has a pungent flavor and stays crisp
Iceberg or crisp head lettuce	A large lettuce with crisp outer leaves and a firm sweet heart. This is the basis of many a salad as the leaves will stay crisp.	Sweet heart, stays crisp
Leaf lettuce	Soft, plain or frilly leaves ranging in color from light green to reddish bronze. Some varieties look like oak leaves!	Slightly bitter
Mustard and cress	Seeds are usually sown together and eaten at the seedling stage. Sold in pints. Snip off the tops as required.	Hot and peppery
Radicchio	Sold in small heads or as tiny single loose leaves either wholly green or tinged with red.	Slightly bitter
Spinach	Dark green smooth or curly leaves. Eaten raw in saladswhen leaves are young and fresh. Stalk may be eaten as well.	Mild
Swiss Chard	Used in salads only when leaves are very young. Discard the white or red stalk. The older, larger leaves should be steamed and eaten hot.	Mild
Watercress	Pick over the bunch using only young leaves and tender stems for salads. Whatever remains will make an excellent soup.	Pungent, slightly peppery

Index